BLUEPRINT FOR TYRANNY

BLUEPRINT FOR TYRANNY
EXECUTIVE ORDER 11490

WESTERN ISLANDS

PUBLISHERS

BOSTON   LOS ANGELES

Introduction

Too few Americans are aware of the impact of Executive Orders. Too few realize that when a President drafts an order, signs it, and publishes it in the Federal Register, it takes on the same weight and muscle as a law passed by Congress. There need be no debate on it in Congress. There is no way for a citizen to express himself about it, or for a Senator to cast a vote against it, or for a newspaper to review the arguments pro or con. An Executive Order just happens — whenever and about whatever the President wishes.

This is precisely what happened when President Nixon signed Executive Order 11490 on October 28, 1969, to be published in the Federal Register two days later. Executive Order 11490 carries the title "Assigning Emergency Preparedness Functions to Federal Departments and Agencies."

Briefly stated, Executive Order 11490 authorizes the plans and assigns the responsibilities for complete takeover by the Government of every facet of life in the United States whenever the President decides that such action is necessary. The Preamble to the body of the Order suggests to a casual reader that such a far-reaching and drastic plan would be implemented only during some immense national catastrophe. However, the document itself says that the plans it orders to be developed are intended for use "in any emergency type situation." Nowhere is this imprecise phrase defined. The definition therefore is left to the discretion of the President. It is because of all these facts that Executive Order 11490 has been labelled a "Blueprint For Tyranny."

After reading the above paragraphs, any normal American

would surely want some quick answers. Is this Executive Order really law? Who can implement it? When? How did the President get such power? And so on. Some have been known to say flatly, "I don't believe it!"

Such questions are a normal response when an American first hears about this Executive Order. Brief answers are provided below; more detailed information and analysis follow, after which will be found the complete text of Executive Order 11490.

Does this Executive Order really have the force of law?

Yes, as long as the Courts and the Congress acquiesce.

By whom and when can the Order be converted from a plan to an actual fact?

If the President decides, on his own responsibility, that the country is in "a national emergency type situation," he can at any time order full implementation of all the plans called for in Executive Order 11490.

Isn't this Order intended for use only during an immense emergency such as a nuclear attack?

Not necessarily. Such a vague and undefined condition as "a national emergency type situation" could be anything from a flood to a continuing rise in inflation or riots in Washington, D.C.

How did the President get so much power?

He and his predecessors assumed it. Congress and the Supreme Court have tacitly agreed to this vast assumption of power by offering no objection to it.

Do the people of the United States have any protection from arbitrary implementation of this Order?

Yes, but the protection will exist only if widespread understanding of the Order and the threat it contains can be created.

The purpose of this book is to create understanding of the Blueprint For Tyranny, and also of a gigantic drive for power that is fastening controls on a free people. Executive Order

11490 is part of that power grab. Not only must this Order be voided but the entire drive for power must be stopped. It cannot be stressed too heavily that a solid understanding of the threat by those who are threatened — the American people — must come before effective action to stop it can follow. Unless understanding provides the foundation for such action, the total threat inherent in the Blueprint For Tyranny will become an established reality.

II

In present usage Executive Orders have the very same force and effect as a bill passed by the Congress and signed into law by the President. The President merely signs the Order and publishes it in the Federal Register, and whatever he has so promulgated is considered to be law. He may later request of Congress that it follow up his order with a Congressionally instituted law covering the same matter; or he may not. If he suspected Congress would not comply, it is probable that he would not. It's all completely up to him.

It should be clearly recognized that the assumed powers inherent in the use of Executive Orders are potentially dictatorial, even tyrannical, and certainly out of keeping with a nation of free men. Yet the situation unfortunately is precisely as described, and both the Legislative branch (the Congress) and the Judicial branch (the Supreme Court) are cooperating with the Executive branch with hardly a whimper of protest.

The issuance of Executive Orders has always been a prerogative of the President. The scope of these orders as originally intended and as used by President Washington and his successors, however, was a great deal more limited than it is today. Originally, their purpose was to facilitate the smooth internal functioning of the Executive branch of the government. Nowhere in the Constitution is any expressed power given to the Executive branch to perform a legislative function.

In fact, Executive Orders were formerly so innocuous that, until 1907, nobody even bothered to keep track of them. As an example of the proper subject matter of these Orders, it is known that George Washington issued an Executive Order on June 8, 1789, which ordered the heads of Executive Departments to submit "a clear account" of affairs connected with their departments. Later, by gradual development, Executive Orders came to be concerned with such things as disposition of the public domain (*e.g.*, withdrawal of lands from federal reservations), promulgation of rules for federal employees (*e.g.*, appointment of postal employees and granting of a day off on Christmas Eve), and "housekeeping" matters not requiring acts of Congress.

Since the Constitution places all law-making power in the Congress, no other body should be in the business of making laws. Executive Orders should not make law, but should be concerned solely with administration of the internal matters of the Executive Departments.

In March 1967, the Legislative Reference Service of the Library of Congress made available a study entitled "Executive Orders — A Brief History of Their Use and The President's Power To Issue Them."[1] The study offers no conclusions but provides some valuable insights. Two statements right at the beginning are worthy of special note: (1) "An Executive Order has never been defined by Congress," and (2) "The validity of Executive Orders has been questioned many times, but a ruling as to the extent or limit to which they may be used has never been determined by the Courts or by Congress." In other words, the whole business is still up in the air and the pathway for abuse has always been open.

The study proceeds to quote statements made by the Courts over the years in opinions rendered in cases involving specific Executive Orders or related matters. As will be shown, the attitude of the Court has shifted from holding strongly that the Executive branch cannot make law to an attitude of indecision and permissiveness regarding excesses such as President Nixon's Executive Order 11490.

Back in 1866, the Court stated in *Ex parte Milligan, 4 Wall 2*:

> The power to make the necessary laws is in the Congress; the power to execute [them] in the President. Both powers imply many subordinate and auxiliary powers. Each includes all authorities essential to its due exercise. But, neither can the President, in war more than peace, intrude upon the proper authority of the Congress, nor Congress upon the proper authority of the President. Both are servants of the people, whose will is expressed in the fundamental law.

In 1926, Justice Brandeis stated in *Myers v. United States, 272 US 240, 293*, the importance of the separation of powers:

> The doctrine of the separation of powers was adopted by the Convention of 1787, not to promote efficiency but to preclude the exercise of arbitrary power. The purpose was, not to avoid friction, but, by means of the inevitable friction incident to the distribution of the governmental powers among these departments, to save the people from autocracy.

In 1952, the Court actually struck down as unconstitutional President Truman's Executive Order seizing the steel industry. In part, its opinion said:

> Nor can the seizure order be sustained because of the several constitutional provisions that grant executive power to the President. In the framework of our Constitution, the President's power to see that the laws are faithfully executed refutes the idea that he is to be a lawmaker.

There is certainly no quarrel with any of the three

preceding opinions. But, by 1959, the Warren Court was looking at the Constitution and the subject of Executive Orders in a new way. In *Greene v. McElroy 360 U.S. 474, 508,* the question dealt with action taken under Executive Orders about the safeguarding of official information. In the opinion of the Court, Chief Justice Warren declared that the Court did not

> ... decide whether the President has inherent authority to create such a program, whether congressional action is necessary, or what the limits on executive or legislative authority may be . . . .

This opened wide a door that was already ajar, and increasing assumption of power by the Executive branch followed. One route to more power, of course, is the use of Executive Orders such as 11490. On the surface, this aptly named "Blueprint For Tyranny" is nothing more than a directive to the various departments within the Executive branch. However, this directive has ordered these departments to involve themselves in purely legislative functions; and not only has it usurped the legislative power of Congress, but it has also ordered these departments to meddle in matters that are reserved to the States.

Not all of the blame for these abuses should be directed at the Warren Court. While an occasional sound statement emanated from previous Courts, they have all, over many years, permitted huge increases in Executive power, through acquiescence.

Congress must also share the blame for the transfer of much of its power to the Executive. Congress has not only allowed but has even fostered the increases in power by the Executive branch. In addition, Congress still holds the purse strings, and it has failed to use its power to refuse appropriations to any unconstitutional federal agency or activity.

One other related matter must be considered. The argument has been advanced that Congress has the power to delegate its legislative authority to the Executive, thereby allowing law to be made by such means as Executive Orders. The clear response must be that Congress, under the Constitution as written, has no authority to delegate its law-making prerogatives to anyone. Nevertheless we know that such delegation is practiced, especially when Congress gives the President power to issue Executive Orders as part of a new law. The Supreme Court has not seen fit to stop this practice, and through its refusal to do so it is failing to maintain the separation of powers so wisely written into the Constitution. The result is that the power to make laws affecting the lives and freedoms of the people of the United States has been assumed by the Executive branch in the person of the President.

Executive Orders like 11490 are not something new with Mr. Nixon but have been with us through a number of administrations. Under Truman and Eisenhower, similar Executive Orders were published assigning substantially the same dictatorial powers to the Civil Defense Administration and the Office of Defense Mobilization. These orders, however, were for use in the single eventuality of military attack. They are not altogether objectionable, inasmuch as it is not unreasonable in such an emergency to lay out a temporary course of action to be coterminous with the emergency.

During the Kennedy Administration, however, a piecemeal transfer of these powers from the Defense-oriented departments to a newly created Office of Emergency Planning was accomplished. Since then it has been possible to bring about implementation of total government power at a moment's notice should an undefined "emergency" occur — which does not have to be caused by a military attack. This remarkable shift from "Defense" to "emergency" has fantastically broadened Executive power. [2]

New Executive Orders which assigned "Emergency Preparedness Functions" to thirty departments and agencies were signed and filed by Presidents Kennedy and Johnson during the years 1961-1966. In each of these Orders, appropriate officials were ordered to prepare "plans and programs . . . designed to develop a state of readiness in these areas with respect to all conditions of national emergency including an attack on the United States." Again, an attack upon the United States is just one condition under which these orders could be made effective.

Further, the Kennedy-Johnson Orders all contained the following language:

> Emergency Action: Nothing in this order shall be construed as conferring authority . . . to put into effect any emergency plan, procedure, policy, program or course of action prepared or developed pursuant to this order. Such authority is reserved to the President.

Or, in simple English, the total rule envisioned by these Executive Orders could not begin until the President gave the word. Implicit in the statement, of course, was the simple corollary that total rule could begin when he *did* give the word. And under these Orders, he could have given that word and implemented total dictatorial control in any event which he chose to designate as a "national emergency" − which is to say, at his own pleasure.

The Orders issued by Presidents Kennedy and Johnson actually gave very general guidelines to the various departments for development of specific plans that would accomplish rationing of power, fuel, food, etc.; takeover of transportation; registration of all persons; mobilization of all persons with medical training; reassignment of all living spaces; seizure of all communication facilities; and on and on. The specific plans developed for each department have never been published. It is obvious, however, that the sky was the limit and that anything up to and including maximum tyranny was permissible.

All of these Executive Orders mandated by Presidents Kennedy and Johnson were finally consolidated into the single Executive Order 11490 by President Nixon in October 1969. This brings us up to date, for it is under this order that we live today.

Executive Order 11490, every bit as inclusive as the previous Executive Orders, follows their pattern exactly. Every department of government is instructed to develop plans and programs, and the sum total of their effect will be to control every facet of life in the United States. For example, the Post Office has been directed to draw up plans to accomplish the registration of persons; the Department of Agriculture, plans to allocate food, farm equipment, etc.; the Department of Labor, plans to mobilize manpower resources; the Department of Transportation and the Civil Aeronautics Board, plans for the takeover and redistribution of all civil aircraft; and on and on. Once again, the specific plans and programs developed by each department in carrying out these directions have not been published.

Following also in the footsteps of its predecessors, President Nixon's Blueprint For Tyranny can be implemented "in any national emergency type situation." As previously noted, there is no definition or explanation of this vague but obviously important phrase. Just as was the case with the Kennedy-Johnson Orders, we can only assume that the interpretation is left solely to the President himself.

It has been erroneously assumed by many that some identifiable emergency must exist and be noted before any President can assume the dictatorial power contained in the Blueprint For Tyranny. Many informed Americans have believed that the proclamation of a real or contrived national emergency would have to be made before this Order could take effect. However, this is not so.

The President need not declare any national emergency because one has already been declared. In fact, a continuous condition of national emergency has existed in the United States since that declared by President Roosevelt during the banking crisis of 1933. The Roosevelt emergency was superseded by another national emergency proclaimed by President Truman in 1950 when the Red Chinese entered the Korean War.

On August 15, 1971, President Nixon ordered wage and price controls, citing as his authority to do so a law passed by Congress in 1970. Little notice was given to his full statement, published the following day, in which he declared "a national emergency." Shortly thereafter, Representative John Rarick (D.-La.) asked in a letter to the President whether the newly proclaimed "national emergency" triggered the implementation of Executive Order 11490. While answering in the negative, John W. Dean III, Counsel to the President, stated: "Since the 1950 emergency declared by President Truman has continued in effect . . . the declaration of August 15 does not significantly change the legal picture from what existed prior to that date."[3] In other words, we have been operating under national emergency conditions for decades, and continue to do so today.

As bad as these Executive Orders are in themselves, we must also realize that vast additional emergency powers have been granted to and assumed by the President. These emergency powers are virtually unlimited in scope and could be given effect at any moment, at the sole discretion of the President, inasmuch as an emergency situation has already been declared to exist. Most of these powers have been granted by Congress and never repealed. It appears that many Congressmen must have voted for the emergency powers these laws confer with a potential military attack in mind.[4]

Occasionally, some of his emergency powers are employed by the President. For instance, in August 1971, at the same time President Nixon instituted wage and price controls, he floated the dollar under emergency provisions of a 1934 Act of Congress that still stands. He also imposed a 10 per cent surcharge on imports under the emergency provisions of a 1962 law that still remains on the books.

Since a condition of national emergency has, by Presidential declaration, existed continuously since 1933, it is not unreasonable to wonder why Mr. Nixon felt it necessary to proclaim another. According to William Rehnquist, then Assistant Attorney General in charge of the Justice Department's Office of Legal Counsel (now a Justice of the Supreme Court), Mr. Nixon's declaration was not necessary and he issued it merely to "focus public attention on the seriousness of the situation." Rehnquist stressed that Mr. Nixon's actions of 1971 involved only "limited" use of his emergency powers, and he further acknowledged that some 200 emergency statutes, plus other similar laws, are still operative.[5]

Therefore, the situation in which we find ourselves is one where the President, through the use of Executive Orders or emergency powers, could assume dictatorial control of our country at will. He could do it without consulting Congress and without the need for any further declaration of national emergency.

No educated guess as to whether President Nixon would ever proclaim such a dictatorship can be made without a review of some recent history and at least the beginning of a realization that many prominent Americans have not had the best interests of our country and ourselves always uppermost in their minds.

III

When the full import of the Blueprint For Tyranny is brought home to anyone, he must decide either to trust the

President or not to trust him. Should he continue living with a trusting reliance that his freedom is secure, or should he become concerned and alarmed about his freedoms? If he decides to trust the President, he must realize that he is placing his own and his children's future and the future of his nation in the President's hands. If he decides not to trust the President, he must immediately realize that in any action he initiates he faces an uphill struggle in which he will be bucking the very well-entrenched Establishment, for his task is nothing less than seeing to it that these vast powers are taken away.

A simple study of human nature suggests that no human being should ever be trusted with the powers already in the hands of the President. In addition, close reading of undistorted recent history should remove any doubt that recent Presidents have acted otherwise than in the best interests of our country and ourselves. Knowledge of human nature and of recent history, therefore, both confirm that the Blueprint For Tyranny is aptly named.

Rather than presume that the reader has been exposed to the information that has caused many Americans increasingly to distrust our leaders, both present and past, let us present a sampling of history for the past thirty years, as we see it. Out of this information has come to others the realization that all is not well, that trusting our leaders is dangerous, and that a man who wishes to remain free had better get busy.

As we look back, a pattern of betrayal can be seen by all but the faint-hearted. The pattern began to take form well before the incidents related here, but we are making no attempt to be completely thorough. We are asking whether such men as those who have recently served as our Presidents should be entrusted with increasingly vast powers.

Let us start with the actions of President Franklin Roosevelt leading to our participation in World War II.

Even before the war was over, it had become painfully evident that he willfully goaded the Japanese into attacking us at Pearl Harbor, and that he and General George C. Marshall had kept news of the impending attack from our forces. The Commanders in Hawaii, General Short and Admiral Kimmel, were disgraced by innuendo and were never given the courts-martial they requested so that their records could be cleared and the truth made known.[6] The thousands who died at Pearl Harbor and in the long war in the Pacific had little knowledge that their sacrifices were arranged to serve a global power scheme. Before too many years had gone by, internationalist-minded proponents of our participation in foreign wars openly praised the "wisdom" of President Roosevelt which resulted in Pearl Harbor and World War II. [7]

Did that President merit your trust?

Poland fell to Communism in 1947. Shortly thereafter our Ambassador to Poland, Arthur Bliss Lane, resigned his post to publish the story of what had happened. His book, *I Saw Poland Betrayed*, detailed the treasonous activity of our State Department which caused Poland to be subverted.[8] Mr. Lane's book caused hardly a ripple of protest because of a very real conspiracy of silence throughout the nation, and especially in official circles. Similarly, our national policy-makers saw to it that anti-Communist Mihailovich of Yugoslavia was destroyed and Communist Tito promoted into power. The same pattern was even more clearly obvious in the fall of China in 1949. When those responsible were called to task by Congressional authorities, President Truman used every possible means to protect the subversives and besmirch the investigators.[9]

Did that President merit your trust?

By 1954, it had become obvious to a number of Americans that the United Nations wanted to absorb the United States into a one-world system run by itself. Senator Robert Taft was one of those who came to see that the U.N. was, as he put it, "a trap." He said, "Let's go it alone!"[10] One means to blunt the drive for U.N. control over our sovereignty was to establish clearly that the provisions of any treaty or international agreement such as the United Nations Treaty, should be subordinate to the United States Constitution and its Bill of Rights. This and other sound safeguards were proposed in the Bricker Amendment. But the good sense evident in the Amendment was not the preference of internationalists in the Senate, who carried the Bricker Amendment to its defeat by a single vote – or of President Eisenhower, who stepped beyond his legitimate executive role in his strong campaign to defeat the Amendment. Mr. Eisenhower, Vice President Nixon, Secretary of State Dulles, and other members of the Executive branch demonstrated their preference for internationalism over the sovereignty of the nation they had sworn to defend.[11]

Did that President and his top aides merit your trust?

The 1960s will always be identified with the Vietnamese war, which carried on the no-win tradition established in Korea in the '50s. Tens of thousands of Americans have given their lives in Vietnam, while the official policy of three successive Presidents has steadfastly demanded that they not win. Meanwhile it has been the official policy of Presidents Kennedy, Johnson, and Nixon to increase as rapidly as possible all types of aid to and trade with the very nations which are supplying the arsenal of the enemy who is killing our men.[12]

Did these Presidents merit your trust?

The United States government, beginning in 1964, has supplied funding, organization, and protection for criminals and subversives of every stripe right here in our own country. The agency responsible for this treasonous activity is the Office of Economic Opportunity (War on Poverty) and its innumerable sub-agencies. Presidents Johnson and Nixon have continually defended the O.E.O., while increasing its subversive activity and scope. [13]

Have they merited your trust?

For thirty years our Presidents and our diplomats have gone all out to hurt our allies and strengthen our enemies. The most recent and horrible example of both sides of this coin was plainly evident when President Nixon journeyed to Peking early in 1972. For all the world to witness, he exchanged felicitations and honors in the name of the American people with the most bloody tyrants in all history. The prestige he gave to them, and the corresponding blow he offered to 750 million captives of the Red Chinese, to our staunch allies in Nationalist China, and to anti-Communists everywhere, mark his action as one of the worst betrayals in recorded history. [14]

Why should President Nixon be trusted to look out for the interests of free men anywhere?

During the Nixon Administration alone, our national indebtedness has climbed more than $100 billion, leaving our currency all but destroyed and the American people reeling under increasing taxation, rising inflation, and economic stagnation. In less than four years President Nixon has accounted for approximately 25 per cent of the total indebtedness of the nation. [15]

President Nixon has moved heaven and earth to cover up the easily proven fact that Red China is flooding our country with heroin — for the avowed purpose of destroying our youth. [16]

During the Nixon years, government has daily increased its size, its scope, and its power. Who can deny it? And who can deny that more and more government can lead to total government, and that we are heading in that direction exactly as many great nations and civilizations have done before us?

It should by now be quite clear that the direction in which we are heading leads to the goal specified in President

Nixon's Executive Order 11490, the Blueprint For Tyranny. Should Richard Nixon be trusted with such power?

IV

For generations, brilliant and ambitious men have been hard at work to establish dominance over the entire globe, A major part of their effort has been directed toward the imposition of tyranny over the United States. As has been shown, the Blueprint For Tyranny is already an accomplished fact. It could be implemented at a moment's notice by the man who is today the chief executive in our land.

A conspiracy is a secret plot to do evil. Conspiracies presuppose hidden activity on the part of more than one individual for a purpose that is objectively wrong.

Having presented only a tiny fraction of the evidence which has convinced many Americans that our country is being victimized by a conspiracy of power-seekers, let us emphatically state our full agreement with their opinion. Further, let us add our belief that the ultimate goal of this conspiracy is world rule and that the present leadership of the United States is party to it.[17] Finally, let us draw the obvious conclusion that the imposition on the United States of totalitarian rule from within is the last step of any consequence remaining before the conspirators' ultimate goal is achieved.

What then of Executive Order 11490? Where does this Blueprint For Tyranny fit into the picture?

There are two ways to achieve total government here in the United States. The first way is the lightning-quick takeover, which could be accomplished by enactment of the Executive Order. The second is the piecemeal acquisition of power, by which all elements of the Blueprint for Tyranny could be accomplished separately in a manner that would also destroy all will to resist.

It has been said that a conquered enemy must be continually reconquered, because he will keep on resisting. A campaign that brings about subversion to such an extent that the victim is induced to beg for his chains will result in a much more secure tyranny.

For this reason especially, it appears obvious that the piecemeal route to tyranny is the choice of the conspiracy; and study of the conspiracy's mode of operation to date seems to confirm this.

Why then have they bothered to publish Executive Order 11490?

Publication of Executive Order 11490 is probably intended to serve a number of purposes. One purpose undoubtedly is to provide a safety switch for the conspiracy should its final goal become unattainable by the chosen means. Obviously, a conspiracy would prefer to establish tyranny over some resistance rather than fail completely. Whenever the plans have been fully developed (and we believe that this has already been accomplished), President Nixon could give the order for full implementation at any time.

Another reason for publishing the Blueprint For Tyranny is probably to allay alarm within government itself. Certainly the Executive Order calls for many actions by many bureaucrats and civil servants which are in themselves quite alarming and upsetting. Since the preponderant majority of government employees are basically patriotic, any one of these individuals, asked to develop plans for, say, deactivation or suspension of broadcasting facilities, might question the reason. Similarly, a minor bureaucrat given the task of formulating procedures for closing the security exchanges and freezing stock and bond prices might refuse, or sound an alarm.

But if all who ask questions about such assignments are shown President Nixon's Executive Order and assured that the plan is for use only in dire national emergency, there is little likelihood that such individuals will question the totalitarian function they are performing.

However, the major reason for the issuance of the Blueprint For Tyranny is its value as a guideline for all federal departments to follow in the piecemeal imposition of tyranny. While each department is setting up the mechanics for a so-called "emergency," the continual piecemeal acquisition of power is proceeding toward a totalitarian state in a real rather than a hypothetical sense.

V

Unless this whole drive for power is exposed and destroyed, a day will soon come when even previously uninformed Americans will realize that all of it has already been accomplished right under their noses, and that resistance would be folly. There will be no lightning-quick seizure of power. None will be needed, for all will have been done in very gradual steps, each of which seemed necessary and reasonable at the time. In the end, total government will be the outcome, and freedom will be gone.

To any skeptics who may not agree with either our premises or our conclusions, let me ask:

Who would have thought that a free people would ever applaud the imposition of wage and price controls over their economy?

Who would have thought that the American people would allow their children to be pawns in a government control scheme called busing?

Who would have thought that American farmers would ever be jailed and fined for planting the "wrong" amount of crops on their own land?

Who would have thought that prayer and Bible reading and even the mention of God could ever be banned from the public schools of America?

Who would have thought that government would take unto itself the right to decide whether unborn infants shall live or die?

And why would any man arrange for publication of the vast powers contained in Executive Order 11490, unless his action served some useful purpose? It would be well for the American people to recall that President Nixon publicly protested when Congress granted him the power to institute wage and price controls. Yet he signed the bill into law — and approximately one year later he used the very power he had earlier said should not be given to anyone.

To those who want to know what to do about the situation in which we find ourselves, and whether or not the drive for total power can be stopped, let me offer the following assessment and suggest a course of action.

The Supreme Court could declare the Blueprint For Tyranny unconstitutional, as it clearly is. The 1952 Court did exactly this when President Truman attempted to seize control of the steel industry by Executive Order. The Supreme Court could also strip the President of all open-ended emergency powers,* which also violate the Constitution. We should reiterate that we are not arguing here against any well-defined and temporary crisis plan to be invoked in the event and for the duration of a military attack.

Since the Supreme Court has been staffed by recent Presidents with like-minded promoters of total government, the chances of their taking the necessary action are so slim as to be just about non-existent. However, none of what has been described can happen without the acquiescence of Congress. Therefore, we believe that the best place to stop the growing tyranny is right here. A sufficient number of informed and patriotic Congressmen can cripple the conspiracy's drive for power. Congress can register an emphatic NO to any further

*Open ended as to when they are to be invoked and as to how long they shall remain in effect.

expansion of government power. It can order the repeal of Executive Order 11490 as it has done in the case of other Executive Orders in the past. It can withhold appropriations from any federal program. It can strip the President of all open-ended emergency powers. And it can force the Supreme Court to cease tinkering with and dismantling the Constitutio.

Congress *can* do all of these things, but the present Congress obviously has no such intention. If your Congressman can't be persuaded to take these actions, then you must work to get a new one.

Among the specific recommendations we think an American citizen should follow are these:

1. Become familiar with the threat to your freedom. Read Executive Order 11490 and realize that the totaliarian controls it envisions are meant for you.

2. Become equally familiar with the solution to the problem, which begins simply with the creation of awareness on the part of your fellow citizens. The ultimate solution is to be found at the polling place on election day, but awareness of the problem must come before any political solution is possible.

3. Work through organizations. The organized few will always succeed where the disorganized continuously fail. The most effective organization for creating awareness of this conspiracy is The John Birch Society.

Above all, be assured that this conspiracy can be turned aside, as can all conspiracies before they have achieved total power. Its progress has been immense, but the conspirators are still short of their goal. A sufficiently dedicated and hard-working handful of Americans can rout them and restore true Constitutional government to our country.

John F. McManus

References

1. Legislative Reference Service Publication No. 398/117-R, A-190, originally issued February 2, 1961, revised March 9, 1967.

2. "Planned Dictatorship," *Dan Smoot Report,* June 3, 1963.

3. Letter to Congressman John Rarick, entered by him in *Congressional Record*, November 2, 1971, Page E11719.

4. "If A President Chose To Use All His Powers," *U.S. News & World Report*, October 25, 1971.

5. "Crisis Powers − A Blank Check For The President," *The Washington Post*, September 5, 1971.

6. R.A. Theobald *The Final Secret Of Pearl Harbor*, New York, Devin-Adair, 1952; Husband E. Kimmel, *Admiral Kimmel's Story*, Chicago, Regnery, 1955; and Charles C. Tansill, *Back Door To War*, Chicago, Regnery, 1951.

7. For example, see Forrest Davis and Ernest K. Lindley, *How War Came*, New York, Simon & Schuster, 1942.

8. Arthur Bliss Lane, *I Saw Poland Betrayed*, New York, The Bobbs-Merrill Company, 1948.

9. Robert Welch, *Again, May God Forgive Us*, Belmont, Mass., Belmont Publishing Co., 1972.

10. Congressman James Utt, Speech in the House of Representatives, January 15, 1962. See Congressional Comment On The U.N., Belmont, Mass., American Opinion.

11. Dean Clarence Manion, *The Conservative American*, Shepardsville, Kentucky, Victor Publishing Co., 1966.

12. Robert Welch, "The Truth About Vietnam" and "More Truth About Vietnam" (pamphlets), Belmont, Mass., American Opinion.

13. Gary Allen, "War On Poverty: Billions To Finance Revolution," *American Opinion*, February 1968.

14. Richard L. Walker, *The Human Cost Of Communism In Red China*, Senate Internal Security Subcommittee, Staff Study, July 1971.

15. Medford Evans, "The Budget: Taxation By Misrepresentation," *American Opinion,* May 1972.

16. John G. Schmitz, "Peking's Narcotics Offensive," *The Review Of The News,* July 19, 1972. 17.

17. Gary Allen, *None Dare Call It Conspiracy,* Rossmoor, California, Concord Press, 1972.

Executive Order 11490

Title 3
THE PRESIDENT
Executive Order 11490
ASSIGNING EMERGENCY PREPAREDNESS FUNCTIONS TO FEDERAL DEPARTMENTS AND AGENCIES

WHEREAS our national security is dependent upon our ability to assure continuity of government, at every level, in any national emergency type situation that might conceivably confront the nation; and

WHEREAS effective national preparedness planning to meet such an emergency, including a massive nuclear attack, is essential to our national survival; and

WHEREAS effective national preparedness planning requires the identification of functions that would have to be performed during such an emergency, the assignment of responsibility for developing plans for performing these functions, and the assignment of responsibility for developing the capability to implement those plans; and

WHEREAS the Congress has directed the development of such national emergency preparedness plans and has provided funds for the accomplishment thereof; and

WHEREAS this national emergency preparedness planning activity has been an established program of the United States Government for more than twenty years:

NOW, THEREFORE, by virtue of the authority vested in

1

me as President of the United States, and pursuant to Reorganization Plan No. 1 of 1958 (72 Stat. 1799), the National Security Act of 1947, as amended, the Defense Production Act of 1950, as amended, and the Federal Civil Defense Act, as amended, it is hereby ordered as follows—

TABLE OF CONTENTS

THE PRESIDENT

Part I

Purpose and Scope

SECTION 101 *Purpose.* This order consolidates the assignment of emergency preparedness functions to various departments and agencies heretofore contained in the 21 Executive orders and 2 Defense Mobilization orders listed in Section 3015 of this order. Assignments have been adjusted to conform to changes in organization which have occurred subsequent to the issuance of those Executive orders and Defense Mobilization orders.

SEC.102 *Scope.* (a) This order is concerned with the emergency national planning and preparedness functions of the several departments and agencies of the Federal Government which complement the military readiness planning responsibilities of the Department of Defense; together, these measures provide the basic foundation for our overall national preparedness posture, and are fundamental to our ability to survive.

(b) The departments and agencies of the Federal Government are hereby severally charged with the duty of assuring the continuity of the Federal Government in any national emergency type situation that might confront the nation. To this end, each department and agency with essential functions, whether expressly identified in this order or not, shall develop such plans and take such actions, including but not limited to those specified in this order, as may be necessary to assure that it will be able to perform its essential functions, and continue as a viable part of the Federal Government, during any emergency that might conceivably occur. These include plans for maintaining the continuity of essential functions of the department or agency at the seat of government and elsewhere, through programs concerned with: (1) succession to office; (2) predelegation of emergency authority; (3) safekeeping of essential records;

3

(4) emergency relocation sites supported by communications and required services; (5) emergency action steps; (6) alternate headquarters or command facilities; and (7) protection of Government resources, facilities, and personnel. The continuity of Government activities undertaken by the departments and agencies shall be in accordance with guidance provided by, and subject to evaluation by, the Director of the Office of Emergency Preparedness.

(c) In addition to the activities indicated above, the heads of departments and agencies described in Parts 2 through 29 of this order shall: (1) prepare national emergency plans, develop preparedness programs, and attain an appropriate state of readiness with respect to the functions assigned to them in this order for all conditions of national emergency; (2) give appropriate consideration to emergency preparedness factors in the conduct of the regular functions of their agencies, particularly those functions considered essential in time of emergency, and (3) be prepared to implement, in the event of an emergency, all appropriate plans developed under this order.

SEC. 103 *Presidential Assistance.* The Director of the Office of Emergency Preparedness, in accordance with the provisions of Executive Order No. 11051 of September 27, 1962, shall advise and assist the President in determining national preparedness goals and policies for the performance of functions under this order and in coordinating the performance of such functions with the total national preparedness program.

SEC. 104 *General and Specific Functions.* The functions assigned by Part 30, General Provisions, apply to all departments and agencies having emergency preparedness responsibilities. Specific functions are assigned to departments and agencies covered in Parts 2 through 29.

SEC. 105 *Construction.* The purpose and legal effect of the assignments contained in this order do not constitute authority to implement the emergency plans prepared pursuant to this order. Plans so developed may be effectuated only in the event that authority for such effectuation is provided by a law enacted by the Congress or by an order or directive issued by the President pursuant to statutes or the Constitution of the United States.

Part 2
Department of State

SECTION 201 *Functions.* The Secretary of State shall prepare national emergency plans and develop preparedness programs to permit modification or expansion of the activities of the Department of State and agencies, boards, and commissions under his jurisdiction in order to meet all conditions of national emergency, including attack upon the United States. The Secretary of State shall provide to all other departments and agencies overall foreign policy direction, coordination, and supervision in the formulation and execution of those emergency preparedness activities which have foreign policy implications, affect foreign relations, or depend directly or indirectly, on the policies and capabilities of the Department of State. The Secretary of State shall develop policies, plans, and procedures for carrying out his responsibilities in the conduct of the foreign relations of the United States under conditions of national emergency, including, but not limited to (1) the formulation and implementation, in consultation with the Department of Defense and other appropriate agencies, and the negotiation of contingency and post-emergency plans with our allies and of the intergovernmental agreements and arrangements required by such plans; (2) formulation, negotiation, and execution of policy affecting the relationships of the United States with neutral States; (3) formulation and execution of political strategy toward hostile or enemy States, including the definition of war objectives and the political means for achieving those objectives; (4) maintenance of diplomatic and consular representation abroad; (5) reporting and advising on conditions overseas which bear upon the national emergency; (6) carrying out or proposing economic measures with respect to other nations, including coordination with the export control functions of the Secretary of Commerce; (7) mutual assistance activities such as ascertaining requirements of the civilian economies of other nations, making recommendations to domestic resource agencies for meeting such requirements, and determining the availability of and making arrangements for obtaining foreign resources required by the United States; (8) providing foreign assistance, including continuous supervision and general direction of authorized economic and military assistance programs, and determination of the value thereof; (9) protection or evacuation of American citizens and nationals abroad and safeguarding their property; (10) protection and/or control of international organization and foreign diplomatic, consular, and other official personnel and property, or other assets, in the United States; (11) documentary control of persons seeking to enter or leave the United States; and (12) regulation and control of exports of items on the munitions list.

Part 3
Department of the Treasury

SECTION 301 *Functions.* The Secretary of the Treasury shall develop policies, plans and procedures for the performance of emergency functions with respect to (1) stabilization aspects of the monetary, credit, and financial system; (2) stabilization of the dollar in relation to foreign currencies; (3) collection of revenue; (4) regulation of financial institutions; (5) supervision of the Federal depository system; (6) direction of transactions in government securities; (7) tax and debt policies; (8) participation in bilateral and multilateral financial arrangements with foreign governments;

(9) regulation of foreign assets in the United States and of foreign financial dealings (in consultation with the Secretaries of State and Commerce); (10) development of procedures for the manufacture and/or issuance and redemption of securities, stamps, coins, and currency; (11) development of systems for the issuance and payment of Treasury checks; (12) maintenance of the central government accounting and financial reporting system; (13) administration of customs laws, tax laws, and laws on control of alcohol, alcoholic beverages, tobacco, and firearms; (14) suppression of counterfeiting and forgery of government securities, stamps, coins, and currency; (15) protection of the President and the Vice President and other designated persons; (16) granting of loans (including participation in or guarantees of loans) for the expansion of capacity, the development of technological processes, or the production of essential material; and (17) to the extent that such functions have not been transferred to the Secretary of Transportation, enforcement of marine inspection and navigation laws.

SEC. 302 *Financial Coordination.* The Secretary shall assume the initiative in developing plans for implementation of national policy on sharing war losses and for the coordination of emergency monetary, credit, and Federal benefit payment programs of those departments and agencies which have responsibilities dependent on the policies or capabilities of the Department.

Part 4
Department of Defense

SECTION 401 *Functions.* In addition to the civil defense functions assigned to the Secretary of Defense by Executive Order No. 10952, the Secretary of Defense shall perform the following emergency preparedness functions:

(1) Provide specific strategic guidance as required for emergency preparedness planning and programming, in-

cluding, for example, guidance regarding such factors as accessibility of foreign sources of supply and estimated shipping loss discounts and aircraft losses in the event of war.

(2) Develop and furnish quantitative and time-phased military requirements for selected end-items, consistent with defined military concepts, and supporting requirements for materials, components, production facilities, production equipment, petroleum, natural gas, solid fuels, electric power, food, transportation, and other services needed to carry out specified Department of Defense current and mobilization procurement, construction, research and development, and production programs. The items and supporting resources to be included in such requirements, the periods to be covered, and the dates for their submission to the appropriate resource agency will be determined by mutual agreement between the Secretary of Defense and the head of the appropriate resource agency.

(3) Advise and assist the Office of Emergency Preparedness in developing a national system of production urgencies.

(4) Advise and assist the Office of Emergency Preparedness in developing a system, in conjunction with the Department of State, for the international allocation of critical materials and products among the United States and the various foreign claimants in the event of an emergency, including an attack on the United States.

(5) Plan for and administer priorities and allocations authority delegated to the Department of Defense. Authorize procurement and production schedules and make allotments of controlled materials pursuant to program determinations of the Office of Emergency Preparedness.

(6) Assist the Department of Commerce and other appropriate agencies in the development of the production and distribution controls plans for use in any period of emergency.

(7) Develop with industry, plans for the procurement and

production of selected military equipment and supplies needed to fulfill emergency requirements, making maximum use of plants in dispersed locations, and, where essential and appropriate, providing for alternative sources of supply in order to minimize the effects of enemy attack.

(8) Develop with industry, plans and programs for minimizing the effect of attack damage to plants producing major items of military equipment and supply.

(9) Recommend to the Office of Emergency Preparedness measures for overcoming potential deficiences in production capacity to produce selected military supplies and equipment needed to fulfill emergency requirements, when necessary measures cannot be effected by the Department of Defense.

(10) Furnish information and recommendations, when requested by the Office of Emergency Preparedness, for purposes of processing applications for defense loans under Title III of the Defense Production Act of 1950, as amended.

(11) Furnish advice and assistance on the utilization of strategic and critical materials in defense production, including changes that occur from time to time.

(12) Analyze problems that may arise in maintaining an adequate mobilization production base in military-product industries and take necessary actions to overcome these problems within the limits of the authority and funds available to the Department of Defense.

(13) Assist the Secretary of Commerce with respect to the identification and evaluation of facilities important to the national defense.

(14) Advise and assist the Office of Emergency Preparedness in the development and review of standards for the strategic location and physical security of industries, services, government, and other activities for which continuing operation is essential to national security, and exercise physical security cognizance over the facilities assigned to him for such purpose.

(15) Develop and operate damage assessment systems and assist the Office of Emergency Preparedness and other departments and agencies in their responsibilities as stated in Section 3002 (2); participate with the Office of Emergency Preparedness in the preparation of estimates of potential damage from enemy attack.

(16) Advise and assist the Office of Emergency Preparedness in the development of over-all manpower policies to be instituted in the event of an emergency, including an attack on the United States, including the provision of information relating to the size and composition of the Armed Forces.

(17) Advise on existing communications facilities and furnish military requirements for commercial communications facilities and services in planning for and in event of an emergency, including an attack on the United States.

(18) Furnish military requirements for all forms of transportation and transportation facilities in planning for and in the event of emergency, including an attack upon the United States.

(19) Assist the Office of Emergency Preparedness in preparation of legislative programs and plans for coordinating nonmilitary support of emergency preparedness programs.

(20) Develop plans and procedures for the Department of Defense utilization of noindustrial facilities in the event of an emergency in order to reduce requirements for new construction and to provide facilities in a minimum period of time.

(21) Advise and assist the Office of Emergency Preparedness in (1) determining what key foreign facilities and operating rights thereto are important to the security of the United States, and (2) obtaining through appropriate channels protection against sabotage.

(22) Develop plans and procedure to carry out Department of Defense responsibilities stated in the National Censorship Agreement between the Department of Defense and the Office of Emergency Preparedness.

(23) Advise and assist the Department of State in planning for the evacuation of dependents from overseas areas, United States teachers and administrators in the overseas dependents schools, and such other United States citizens as may be working in United States schools overseas.

(24) Develop plans for implementation of approved Department of State/Department of Defense policies and procedures for the protection and evacuation of United States citizens and certain designated aliens abroad.

(25) Develop plans and procedures for the provision of logistical support to members of foreign forces, their employees and dependents as may be present in the United States under the terms of bilateral or multilateral agreements which authorize such support in the event of a national emergency.

(26) Develop with the Department of Transportation and Federal Communications Commission plans and programs for the control of air traffic, civil and military, during an emergency.

(27) Develop with the Federal Communications Commission and the Office of Telecommunications Management (OEP) plans and programs for the emergency control of all devices capable of emitting electromagnetic radiation.

Part 5
Department of Justice

SECTION 501. *Functions.* The Attorney General shall perform the following emergency preparedness functions:

(1) Emergency documents and measures. Provide advice, as appropriate, with respect to any emergency directive or procedure prepared by a department or agency as a part of its emergency preparedness function.

(2) *Industry support.* As appropriate, review the legal procedures developed by the Federal agencies concerned to be instituted if it becomes necessary for the Government to institute extraordinary measures with respect to vital produc-

11

tion facilities, public facilities, communications systems, transportation systems, or other facility, system, or service essential to national survival.

(3) *Judicial and legislative liaison.* In cooperation with the Office of Emergency Preparedness, maintain liaison with Federal courts and with the Congress so there will be mutual understanding of Federal emergency plans involving law enforcement and the exercise of legal powers during emergencies of various magnitudes.

(4) *Legal advice.* Develop emergency plans for providing legal advice to the President, the Cabinet, and the heads of Executive departments and agencies wherever they may be located in an emergency, and provide emergency procedures for the review as to form and legality of Presidential proclamations, Executive orders, directives, regulations, and documents, and of other documents requiring approval by the President or by the Attorney General which may be issued by authorized officers after an armed attack.

(5) *Alien control and control of entry and departure.* Develop emergency plans for the control of alien enemies and other aliens within the United States, and in consultation with the Department of State and Department of the Treasury, develop emergency plans for the control of persons attempting to enter or leave the United States. These plans shall specifically include provisions for the following:

(a) The location, restraint, or custody of alien enemies.

(b) Temporary detention of alien enemies and other persons attempting to enter the United States pending determination of their admissibility.

(c) Apprehension of deserting alien crewmen and stowaways.

(d) Investigation and control of aliens admitted as contract laborers.

(e) Control of persons entering or departing from the United States at designated ports of entry.

(f) Increased surveillance of the borders to preclude prohibited crossings by persons.

(6) *Alien property.* Develop emergency plans, in consultation with the Department of State, for the seizure and administration of property of alien enemies under provisions of the Trading with the Enemy Act.

(7) *Security standards.* In consultation with the Department of Defense and with other executive agencies, to the extent appropriate, prepare plans for adjustment of security standards governing the employment of Federal personnel and Federal contractors in an emergency.

(8) *Drug Control.* Develop emergency plans and procedures for the administration of laws governing the import, manufacture, and distribution of narcotics. Consult with and render all possible aid and assistance to the Office of Emergency Preparedness, the Department of Health, Education, and Welfare, and the General Services Administration in the allocation, distribution, and, if necessary, the replenishment of Government stockpiles of narcotic drugs.

SEC. 502 *Civil Defense Functions.* In consonance with national civil defense programs developed by the Department of Defense, the Attorney General shall:

(1) *Local law enforcement.* Upon request, consult with and assist the Department of Defense to plan, develop, and distribute materials for use in the instruction and training of law enforcement personnel for civil defense emergency operations; develop and carry out a national plan for civil defense instruction and training for enforcement officers, designed to utilize to the maximum extent practicable the resources and facilities of existing Federal, State, and local public schools. academies, and other appropriate institutions of learning; and assist the States in preparing for the conduct of intrastate and interstate law enforcement operations to meet the extraordinary needs that would exist for emergency police services under conditions of attack or imminent attack.

(2) *Penal and correctional institutions.* Develop emergency plans and procedures for the custody and protection of prisoners and the use of Federal penal and correctional institutional resources, when available, for cooperation with local authorities in connection with mass feeding and housing, for the storage of standby emergency equipment, for the emergency use of prison hospitals and laboratory facilities, for the continued availability of prison-industry products, and, in coordination with the Department of Labor, for the development of Federal prisoner skills to appropriately augment the total supply of manpower, advise States and their political subdivisions regarding the use of State and local prisons, jails, and prisoners for the purpose of relieving local situations and conditions arising from a state of emergency.

(3) *Identification and location of persons.* Develop emergency plans and procedures for the use of the facilities and personnel of the Department of Justice in assisting the Department of Health, Education, and Welfare with the development of plans and procedures for the identification of the dead and the reuniting of families during a civil defense emergency.

Part 6
Post Office Department

SECTION 601 *Functions.* The Postmaster General shall prepare plans and programs for emergency mail service and shall cooperate with indicated Federal agencies, in accordance with existing agreements or directives, in the following national emergency programs:

(1) *Registering of persons.* Assist the Department of Health, Education, and Welfare in planning a national program and developing technical guidance for States, and directing Post Office activities concerned with registering persons and families for the purpose of receiving and answering welfare inquiries and reuniting families in civil defense

14

emergencies. The program shall include procurement, transportation, storage, and distribution of safety notification and emergency change of address cards in quantities and localities jointly determined by the Department of Defense and the Post Office Department.

(2) *Other emergency programs.* (a) Censorship of international mails. (Department of Defense; Department of the Treasury; Office of Emergency Preparedness)

(b) Provision for emergency mail service to Federal agencies at both regular and emergency sites. (General Services Administration)

(c) Emergency registration of Federal employees. (Civil Service Commission)

(d) Emergency leasing of space for Federal agencies. (General Services Administration)

(3) Registration of enemy aliens. (Department of Justice)

Part 7
Department of the Interior

SECTION 701 *Résumé of Responsibilities.* The Secretary of the Interior shall prepare national emergency plans and develop preparedness programs covering (1) electric power; (2) petroleum and gas; (3) solid fuels; (4) minerals; and (5) water, as defined in Section 702 of this part.

SEC. 702 *Definitions.* As used in this part:

(1) "Electric power" means all forms of electric power and energy, including the generation, transmission, distribution, and utilization thereof.

(2) "Petroleum" means crude oil and synthetic liquid fuel, their products, and associated hydrocarbons, including pipelines for their movement and facilities specially designed for their storage.

(3) "Gas" means natural gas (including helium) and manufactured gas, including pipelines for their movement and facilities specially designed for their storage.

(4) "Solid fuels" means all forms of anthracite, bituminous, sub-bituminous, and lignitic coals, coke, and coal chemicals produced in the coke-making process.

(5) "Minerals" means all raw materials of mineral origin (except petroleum, gas, solid fuels, and source materials as defined in the Atomic Energy Act of 1954, as amended) obtained by mining and like operations and processed through the stages specified and at the facilities designated in an agreement between the Secretary of the Interior and the Secretary of Commerce as being within the emergency preparedness responsibilities of the Secretary of the Interior.

(6) "Water" means water from all sources except water after its withdrawal into a community system, or an emergency system for treatment, storage, and distribution for public use.

SEC. 703 *Resource functions.* With respect to the resources defined in Section 702, the Secretary of the Interior shall:

(1) *Minerals development.* Develop programs and encourage the exploration, development, and mining of strategic and critical minerals for emergency purposes.

(2) *Production.* Provide guidance and leadership to assigned industries in the development of plans and programs to insure the continuity of production in the event of an attack, and cooperate with the Department of Commerce in the identification and evaluation of essential facilities.

(3) *Water.* Develop plans with respect to water, including plans for the treatment and disposal, after use, of water after its withdrawal into a community system or an emergency system for treatment, storage, and distribution for public use. In developing any plans relating to water for use on farms and in food facilities, assure that those plans are in consonance with plans and programs of the Department of Agriculture.

(4) *Electric power and natural gas.* In preparedness planning for electric power and natural gas, the Federal Power

Commission shall assist the Secretary of the Interior as set forth in Section 1901 of this order.

Part 8
Department of Agriculture

SECTION 801 *Résumé of Responsibilities.* The Secretary of Agriculture shall prepare national emergency plans and develop preparedness programs covering: (1) food resources, farm equipment, fertilizer, and food resource facilities as defined below; (2) lands under the jurisdiction of the Secretary of Agriculture; (3) rural fire control; (4) defense against biological and chemical warfare and radiological fallout pertaining to agricultural activities; and (5) rural defense information and education.

SEC. 802 *Definitions.* As used in this part:

(1) "Food resources" means all commodities and products, simple, mixed, or compound, or complements to such commodities or products, that are capable of being eaten or drunk, by either human beings or animals, irrespective of other uses to which such commodities or products may be put, at all stages of processing from the raw commodity to the products thereof in vendible form for human or animal consumption. For the purposes of this order, the term "food resources" shall also include all starches, sugars, vegetable and animal fats and oils, cotton, tobacco, wool, mohair, hemp, flax fiber, and naval stores, but shall not include any such material after it loses its identity as an agricultural commodity or agricultural product.

(2) "Farm equipment" means machinery, equipment, and repair parts manufactured primarily for use on farms in connection with the production or preparation for market or use of "food resources."

(3) "Fertilizer" means any product or combination of products for plant nutrition in form for distribution to the users thereof.

17

(4) "Food resource facilities" means plants, machinery, vehicles (including on farm), and other facilities (including farm housing) for the production, processing, distribution, and storage (including cold storage) of food resources, and for domestic distribution of farm equipment and fertilizer.

SEC. 803 *Functions.* With respect to food resources, food resource facilities, lands under the jurisdiction of the Secretary, farm equipment, and fertilizer, the Secretary of Agriculture shall:

(1) *Production, processing, storage, and distribution.* Develop plans for priorities, allocations, and distribution control systems and related plans, including control of use of facilities designed to provide adequate and continuing production, processing, storage, and distribution of essential food resources in an emergency, and to provide for the domestic distribution of farm equipment and fertilizer.

(2) *Stockpiles.* In addition to the food stockpile functions identified in Executive Order No. 10958, take all possible measures in the administration of Commodity Credit Corporation inventories of food resources to assure the availability of such inventories when and where needed in an emergency. The Secretary shall also develop plans and procedures for the proper utilization of agricultural items stockpiled for survival purposes.

(3) *Land management.* Develop plans and direct activities for the emergency protection, management, and utilization of the lands, resources, and installations under the jurisdiction of the Secretary of Agriculture and assist in the development of plans for the emergency operation, production, and processing of forest products in cooperation with other Federal, State, and private agencies.

SEC. 804 *Civil Defense Functions.* In consonance with national civil defense programs developed by the Department of Defense, the Secretary of Agriculture shall:

(1) *Rural fire defense.* In cooperation with Federal, State,

and local agencies, develop plans for a national program and direct activities relating to the prevention and control of fires in the rural areas of the United States caused by the effects of enemy attack.

(2) *Biological, chemical, and radiological warfare defense.* Develop plans for a national program, direct Federal activities, and furnish technical guidance to State and local authorities concerning (a) diagnosis and strengthening of defensive barriers and control or eradication of diseases, pests, or chemicals introduced as agents of biological or chemical warfare against animals, crops, or products thereof; (b) protective measures, treatment, and handling of livestock, including poultry, agricultural commodities on farms or ranches, agricultural lands, forest lands, and water for agricultural purposes, any of which have been exposed to or affected by radiation. Plans shall be developed for a national program and direction of Federal activities to assure the safety and wholesomeness and to minimize losses from biological and chemical warfare, radiological effects, and other emergency hazards of livestock, meat and meat products, poultry and poultry products in establishments under the continuous inspection of the Department of Agriculture, and agricultural commodities and products owned by the Commodity Credit Corporation or by the Department of Agriculture.

(3) *Defense information and education.* Conduct a defense information and education program in support of the Department's emergency responsibilities.

Part 9
Department of Commerce
SECTION 901 *Résumé of Responsibilities.* The Secretary of Commerce shall prepare national emergency plans and develop preparedness programs covering:

(1) The production and distribution of all materials, the

19

use of all production facilities (except those owned by, controlled by, or under the jurisdiction of the Department of Defense or the Atomic Energy Commission), the control of all construction materials, and the furnishing of basic industrial services except those involving the following:

(a) Production and distribution of and use of facilities for petroleum, solid fuels, gas, electric power, and water;

(b) Production, processing, distribution, and storage of food resources and the use of food resource facilities for such production, processing, distribution, and storage;

(c) Domestic distribution of farm equipment and fertilizer;

(d) Use of communications services and facilities, housing and lodging facilities, and health, education, and welfare facilities;

(e) Production, and related distribution, of minerals as defined in Subsection 702 (5), and source materials as defined in the Atomic Energy Act of 1954, as amended; and the construction and use of facilities designated as within the responsibilities of the Secretary of the Interior;

(f) Distribution of items in the supply systems of, or controlled by, the Department of Defense and the Atomic Energy Commission;

(g) Construction, use, and management of civil aviation facilities; and

(h) Construction and use of highways, streets, and appurtenant structures.

(2) Federal emergency operational control responsibilities with respect to ocean shipping, ports, and port facilities, except those owned by, controlled by, or under the jurisdiction of the Department of Defense, and except those responsibilities of the Department of the Treasury with respect to the entrance and clearance of vessels. The following definitions apply to this part:

(a) "Ocean shipping" includes all overseas, coastwise, intercoastal, and Great Lakes shipping except that solely engaged in the transportation of passengers and cargo between United States ports on the Great Lakes.

(b) "Port" or "port area" includes any zone contiguous to or associated in the traffic network of an ocean or Great Lakes port, or outport location, including beach loading sites, within which facilities exist for transshipment of persons and property between domestic carriers and carriers engaged in coastal, intercoastal, and overseas transportation.

(c) "Port facilities" includes all port facilities, port equipment including harbor craft, and port services normally used in accomplishing the transfer or interchange of cargo and passengers between ocean-going vessels and other media of transportation, or in connection therewith (including the Great Lakes).

(3) Scientific and technological services and functions, essential to emergency preparedness plans, programs, and operations of the Federal departments and agencies, in which the Department of Commerce has the capability, including, but not limited to:

(a) Meteorological and related services;

(b) Preparation, reproduction, and distribution of nautical and aeronautical charts, geodetic, hydrographic, and oceanographic data, and allied services for nonmilitary purposes;

(c) Standards of measurement and supporting services; and

(d) Research, development, testing, evaluation, application, and associated services and activities in the various fields and disciplines of science and technology in which the Department has special competence.

(4) Collection, compilation, and reporting of census information and the provision of statistical and related services, as required, for emergency planning and operations.

(5) Regulation and control of exports and imports, under the jurisdiction of the Department of Commerce, in support of national security, foreign policy, and economic stabilization objectives.

(6) Regulation and control of transfers of capital to, and reinvestment of earnings of, affiliated foreign nationals pursuant to authority conferred by Executive Order No. 11387 of January 1, 1968.

SEC. 902 *Production Functions.* Within the areas designated in section 901 (1) hereof, the Secretary of Commerce shall:

(1) *Priorities and allocations.* Develop control systems for priorities, allocation, production, and distribution, including provisions for other Federal departments and agencies, as appropriate, to serve as allotting agents for materials and other resources made available under such systems for designated programs and the construction and operation of facilities assigned to them.

(2) *New construction.* Develop procedures by which new production facility construction proposals will be reviewed for appropriate location in light of such area factors as locational security, availability of labor, water, power, housing, and other support requirements.

(3) *Industry evaluation.* Identify and evaluate the national security essentiality of those products and services, and their producing or supporting facilities, which are of exceptional importance to mobilization readiness, national defense, or post-attack survival and recovery.

(4) *Production capability.* Analyze potential effects of attack on actual production capability, taking into account the entire production complex, including shortages of resources, and conduct studies as a basis for recommending pre-attack measures that would strengthen capabilities for post-attack production.

(5) *Loans for plant modernization.* Develop plans, in coordination with the Small Business Administration, for providing emergency assistance to essential small business establishments through direct loans or participation loans for the financing of production facilities and equipment.

SEC. 903 *Maritime Functions.* Within the areas designated

22

in section 901(2) of this part, the Secretary of Commerce shall develop plans and procedures in consonance with international treaties, under coordinating authority of the Secretary of Transportation and in cooperation with other appropriate Federal agencies and the States and their political subdivisions, to provide for Federal operational control of ocean ports and shipping, including:

(1) *Shipping allocation.* Allocation of specific ocean shipping to meet the national requirements, including those for military, foreign assistance, emergency procurement programs, and those essential to the civilian economy.

(2) *Ship acquisition.* Provision of ships for ocean shipping by purchase, charter, or requisition, by breakout from the national defense reserve fleet, and by construction.

(3) *Operations.* Operation of ocean shipping, directly or indirectly.

(4) *Traffic control.* Provisions for the control of passengers and cargo through port areas to assure an orderly and continuous flow of such traffic.

(5) *Traffic priority.* Administration of priorities for the movement of passengers and cargo through port areas.

(6) *Port allocation.* Allocation of specific ports and port facilities to meet the needs of the Nation and our allies.

(7) *Support activities.* Performance of supporting activities needed to carry out the above-described functions, such as: ascertaining national support requirements for ocean shipping, including those for support of military and other Federal programs and those essential to the civil economy; maintenance, repair, and arming of ships; recruiting, training, and assigning of officers and seamen; procurement, warehousing, and issuance of ships' stores, supplies, equipment, and spare parts; supervision of stevedoring and bunkering; management of terminals, shipyards, repair, and other facilities; and provision, maintenance, and restoration of port facilities.

SEC. 904 *Census Functions.* Within the area designated in section 901(4) hereof, the Secretary of Commerce shall:

(1) Provide for the collection and reporting of census information on the status of human and economic resources, including population, housing, agriculture, manufacture, mineral industries, business, transportation, foreign trade, construction, and governments, as required for emergency planning purposes.

(2) Plan, create, and maintain a capability for the conduct of post-attack surveys to provide information on the status of surviving populations and resources as required for the programs of the Office of Emergency Preparedness.

(3) Provide for and maintain the ability to make estimates of attack effects on industry, population, and other resources for use within the Department of Commerce.

SEC. 905 *Civil Defense Functions.* In consonance with national civil defense programs developed by the Department of Defense, the Secretary of Commerce shall:

(1) *Weather functions.* Prepare and issue currently, as well as in an emergency, forecasts and estimates of areas likely to be covered by radiological fallout in event of attack and make this information available to Federal, State, and local authorities for public dissemination.

(2) *Geodetic, hydrographic, and oceanographic data.* Provide geodetic, hydrographic, and oceanographic data and services to the Department of Defense and other governmental agencies, as appropriate.

Part 10
Department of Labor

SECTION 1001 *Résumé of Responsibilities.* The Secretary of Labor shall have primary responsibility for preparing national emergency plans and developing preparedness programs covering civilian manpower mobilization, more effective utilization of limited manpower resources, including specialized personnel, wage and salary stabilization, worker incentives and protection, manpower resources and requirements, skill development and training, research, labor-management relations, and critical occupations.

SEC. 1002 *Functions.* The Secretary of Labor shall:

(1) *Civilian manpower mobilization.* Develop plans and issue guidance designed to utilize to the maximum extent civilian manpower resources, such plans and guidance to be developed with the active participation and assistance of the States and local political subdivisions thereof, and of other organizations and agencies concerned with the mobilization of the people of the United States. Such plans shall include, but not necessarily be limited to:

(a) *Manpower management.* Recruitment, selection and referral, training, employment stabilization (including appeals procedures), proper utilization, and determination of the skill categories critical to meeting the labor requirements of defense and essential civilian activities;

(b) *Priorities.* Procedures for translating survival and production urgencies into manpower priorities to be used as guides for allocating available workers; and

(c) *Improving mobilization base.* Programs for more effective utilization of limited manpower resources, and, in cooperation with other appropriate agencies, programs for recruitment, training, allocation, and utilization of persons possessing specialized competence or aptitude in acquiring such competence.

(2) *Wage and salary stabilization.* Develop plans and procedures for wage and salary stabilization and for the national and field organization necessary for the administration of such a program in an emergency, including investigation, compliance, and appeals procedures; statistical studies of wages, salaries, and prices for policy decisions and to assist operating stabilization agencies to carry out their functions.

(3) *Worker incentives and protection.* Develop plans and

procedures for wage and salary compensation and death and disability compensation for authorized civil defense workers and, as appropriate, measures for unemployment payments, re-employment rights, and occupational safety, and other protection and incentives for the civilian labor force during an emergency.

(4) *Skill development and training.* Initiate current action programs to overcome or offset present or anticipated manpower deficiencies, including those identified as a result of resource and requirements studies.

(5) *Labor-management relations.* Develop, after consultation with the Department of Commerce, the Department of Transportation, the Department of Defense, the National Labor Relations Board, the Federal Mediation and Conciliation Service, the National Mediation Board, and other appropriate agencies and groups, including representatives of labor and management, plans and procedures, including organization plans, for the maintenance of effective labor-management relations during a national emergency.

Part 11
Department of Health, Education, and Welfare

SECTION 1101 *Résumé of Responsibilities.* In addition to the medical stockpile functions identified in Executive Order No. 10958, the Secretary of Health, Education, and Welfare shall prepare national emergency plans and develop preparedness programs covering health services, civilian health manpower, health resources, welfare services, social security benefits, credit union operations, and educational programs as defined below.

SEC.1102 *Definitions.* As used in this part:

(1) "Emergency health services" means medical and dental care for the civilian population in all of their specialties and adjunct therapeutic fields, and the planning, provision, and

26

operation of first aid stations, hospitals, and clinics; preventive health services, including detection, identification and control of communicable diseases, their vectors, and other public health hazards, inspection and control of purity and safety of food, drugs, and biologicals; vital statistics services; rehabilitation and related services for disabled survivors; preventive and curative care related to human exposure to radiological, chemical, and biological warfare agents; sanitary aspects of disposal of the dead; food and milk sanitation; community solid waste disposal; emergency public water supply; and the determination of the health significance of water pollution and the provision of other services pertaining to health aspects of water use and water-borne wastes as set forth in an agreement between the Secretary of Health, Education, and Welfare and the Secretary of the Interior, approved by the President, pursuant to Reorganization Plan No. 2 of 1966, which plan placed upon the Secretary of the Interior responsibilities for the prevention and control of water pollution. It shall be understood that health services for the purposes of this order, however, do not encompass the following areas for which the Department of Agriculture has responsibility: plant and animal diseases and pest prevention, control, and eradication, wholesomeness of meat and meat products, and poultry and poultry products in establishments under continuous inspection service by the Department of Agriculture, veterinary biologicals, agricultural commodities and products owned by the Commodity Credit Corporation or the Secretary of Agriculture, livestock, agricultural commodities stored or harvestable on farms and ranches, agricultural lands and water, and registration of pesticides.

"Health manpower" means physicians (including osteopaths); dentists; sanitary engineers; registered professional nurses; and such other occupations as may be included in the List of Health Manpower Occupations issued for the purposes of this part by the Director of the Office of Emergency Preparedness after agreement by the Secretary of Labor and the Secretary of Health, Education, and Welfare.

(3) "Health resources" means manpower, material, and facilities required to prevent the impairment of, improve, and restore the physical and mental health conditions of the civilian population.

(4) "Emergency welfare services" means feeding; clothing; lodging in private and congregate facilities; registration; locating and reuniting families; care of unaccompanied children, the aged, the handicapped, and other groups needing specialized care or services; necessary financial or other assistance; counseling and referral services to families and individuals; aid to welfare institutions under national emergency or post-attack conditions; and all other feasible welfare aid and services to people in need during a civil defense emergency. Such measures include organization, direction, and provision of services to be instituted before attack, in the event of strategic or tactical evacuation, and after attack in the event of evacuation or of refuge in shelters.

(5) "Social security benefits" means the determination of entitlement and the payment of monthly insurance benefits to those eligible, such as workers who have retired because of age or disability and to their dependent wives and children, and to the eligible survivors of deceased workers. It also includes determinations of eligibility and payments made on behalf of eligible individuals to hospitals, home health agencies, extended care facilities, physicians, and other providers of medical services.

(6) "Credit union operations" means the functions of any credit union, chartered either by a State or the Federal Government, in stimulating systematic savings by members, the investment and protection of those savings, providing loans for credit union members at reasonable rates, and encouraging sound credit and thrift practices among credit union members.

(7) "Education" or "training" means the organized process of learning by study and instruction primarily through public and private systems.

SEC. 1103 *Health Functions.* With respect to emergency health services, as defined above, and in consonance with national civil defense plans, programs, and operation of the Department of Defense under Executive Order No. 10952, the Secretary of Health, Education, and Welfare shall:

(1) *Professional training.* Develop and direct a nationwide program to train health manpower both in professional and technical occupational content and in civil defense knowledge and skills. Develop and distribute health education material for inclusion in the curricula of schools, colleges, professional schools, government schools, and other educational facilities throughout the United States. Develop and distribute civil defense information relative to health services to States, voluntary agencies, and professional groups.

(2) *Emergency public water supply.* Prepare plans to assure the provision of usable water supplies for human consumption and other essential community uses in an emergency. This shall include inventorying existing community water supplies, planning for other alternative sources of water for emergency uses, setting standards relating to human consumption, and planning community distribution. In carrying on these activities, the Department shall have primary responsibility but will make maximum use of the resources and competence of State and local authorities, the Department of the Interior, and other Federal agencies.

(3) *Radiation.* Develop and coordinate programs of radiation measurement and assessment as may be necessary to carry out the responsibilities involved in the provision of emergency health services.

(4) *Biological and chemical warfare.* Develop and coordinate programs for the prevention, detection, and identification of human exposure to chemical and biological warfare

agents as may be necessary to carry out the responsibilities involved in the provision of emergency health services, including the provision of guidance and consultation to Federal, State, and local authorities on measures for minimizing the effects of biological or chemical warfare.

(5) *Food, drugs, and biologicals.* Plan and direct national programs for the maintenance of purity and safety in the manufacture and distribution of food, drugs, and biologicals in an emergency.

(6) *Disabled survivors.* Prepare national plans for emergency operations of vocational rehabilitation and related agencies, and for measures and resources necessary to rehabilitate and make available for employment those disabled persons among the surviving population.

SEC. 1104 *Welfare Functions.* With respect to emergency welfare services as defined above, and in consonance with national civil defense plans, programs, and operations of the Department of Defense under Executive Order No. 10952, the Secretary of Health, Education, and Welfare shall:

(1) *Federal support.* Cooperate in the development of Federal support procedures, through joint planning with other Departments and agencies, including but not limited to the Post Office Department, the Department of Labor, and the Selective Service System, the Department of Housing and Urban Development, and resource agencies, including the Department of Agriculture, the Department of the Interior, and the Department of Commerce, for logistic support of State and community welfare services in an emergency.

(2) *Emergency welfare training.* Develop and direct a nationwide program to train emergency welfare manpower for the execution of the functions set forth in this part, develop welfare educational materials, including self-help program materials for use with welfare organizations and professional schools, and develop and distribute civil defense

information relative to emergency welfare services to States, voluntary agencies, and professional groups.

(3) *Financial aid.* Develop plans and procedures for financial assistance to individuals injured or in want as a result of enemy attack and for welfare institutions in need of such assistance in an emergency.

(4) *Non-combatant evacuees to the Continental United States.* Develop plans and procedures for assistance, at ports of entry to U.S. personnel evacuated from overseas areas, their onward movement to final destination, and follow-up assistance after arrival at final destination.

SEC. 1105 *Social Security Functions.* With respect to social security, the Secretary of Helath, Education, and Welfare shall:

(1) *Social security benefits.* Develop plans for the continuation or restoration of benefit payments to those on the insurance rolls as soon as possible after a direct attack upon the United States, and prepare plans for the acceptance and disposition of current claims for social security benefits.

(2) *Health insurance.* Develop plans for the payment of health insurance claims for reimbursement for items or services provided by hospitals, physicians, and other providers of medical services submitted by or on behalf of individuals who are eligible under the Medicare program.

SEC. 1106 *Credit Union Functions.* With respect to credit union functions, the Secretary of Health, Education, and Welfare shall:

(1) *Credit union operations.* Provide instructions to all State and Federally chartered credit unions for the development of emergency plans to be put into effect as soon as possible after an attack upon the United States in order to guarantee continuity of credit union operations.

(2) *Economic stabilization.* Provide guidance to credit unions that will contribute to stabilization of the Nation's economy by helping to establish and maintain a sound

economic base for combating inflation, maintaining confidence in public and private financial institutions, and promoting thrift.

SEC. 1107 *Education Functions.* With respect to education, the Secretary of Health, Education, and Welfare shall:

(1) *Program guidance.* Develop plans and issue guidance for the continued function of educational systems under all conditions of national emergency. Although extraordinary circumstances may require the temporary suspension of education, plans should provide for its earliest possible resumption.

(2) *Educational adjustment.* Plan to assist civilian educational institutions, both public and private, to adjust to demands laid upon them by a large expansion of government activities during any type of emergency. This includes advice and assistance to schools, colleges, universities, and other educational institutions whose facilities may be temporarily needed for Federal, State, or local government programs in an emergency or whose faculties and student bodies may be affected by the demands of a sudden or long-standing emergency.

(3) *Post-attack recovery.* Develop plans for the rapid restoration and resumption of education at all levels after an attack. This includes assistance to educators and educational institutions to locate and use surviving facilities, equipment, supplies, books, and educational personnel. Particular emphasis shall be given to the role of educational institutions and educational leadership in reviving education and training in skills needed for post-attack recovery.

(4) *Civil defense education.* In consonance with national civil defense plans, programs, and operations of the Department of Defense, develop and issue instructional materials to assist schools, colleges, and other educational institutions to incorporate emergency protective measures and civil defense concepts into their programs. This includes assistance to

various levels of education to develop an understanding of the role of the individual, family, and community for civil defense in the nuclear age.

Part 12
Department of Housing and Urban Development

SECTION 1201 *Résumé of Responsibilities.* The Secretary of Housing and Urban Development shall prepare national emergency plans and develop preparedness programs covering all aspects of housing, community facilities related to housing, and urban development (except that housing assets under the jurisdiction and control of the Department of Defense, other than those leased for terms not in excess of one year, shall be and remain the responsibility of the Department of Defense).

SEC. 1202 *Definition.* As used in this part:

(1) "Emergency housing" means any and all types of accommodations used as dwellings in an emergency.

(2) "Community facilities related to housing" means installations necessary to furnish water, sewer, electric, and gas services between the housing unit or project and the nearest practical source or servicing point.

(3) "Urban development" means the building or restoration of urban community, suburban, and metropolitan areas (except transportation facilities).

SEC. 1203 *Housing and Community Facilities Functions.* The Secretary of Housing and Urban Development shall:

(1) *New housing.* Develop plans for the emergency construction and management of new housing and the community facilities related thereto to the extent that it is determined that it may be necessary to provide for such construction and management with public funds and through direct Federal action, and to the extent that such construction of new housing may have to be provided through Federal financial or credit assistance.

(2) *Community facilities.* Develop plans to restore community facilities related to housing affected by an emergency through the repair of damage, the construction of new facilities, and the use of alternate or back-up facilities.

SEC. 1204 *Urban Development Functions.* The Secretary of Housing and Urban Development shall:

(1) *Regional cooperation.* Encourage regional emergency planning and cooperation among State and local governments with respect to problems of housing and metropolitan development.

(2) *Vulnerability and redevelopment.* In cooperation with the Office of Emergency Preparedness, develop criteria and provide guidance for the design and location of housing and community facilities related to housing to minimize the risk of loss under various emergency situations. Develop criteria for determining which areas should be redeveloped in the event of loss or severe damage resulting from emergencies.

SEC. 1205 *Civil Defense Functions.* In consonance with national civil defense plans, programs, and operations of the Department of Defense under Executive Order No. 10952, the Secretary of Housing and Urban Development shall:

(1) *Transitional activities.* Develop plans for the orderly transfer of people from fallout shelters and from billets to temporary or permanent housing, including advice and guidance for State and local government agencies in the administration thereof. These plans shall be coordinated with national plans and guidance for emergency welfare services of the Department of Health, Education, and Welfare.

(2) *Temporary housing.* Develop plans for the emergency repair and restoration for use of damaged housing, for the construction and management of emergency housing units and the community facilities related thereto, for the emergency use of tents and trailers, and for the emergency conversion for dwelling use of non-residential structures, such activities to be financed with public funds through direct

34

Federal action or through financial or credit assistance.

(3) *Shelter.* In conformity with national shelter policy assist in the development of plans to encourage the construction of shelters for both old and new housing, and develop administrative procedures to encourage the use of low-cost design and construction techniques to maximize protection in connection with national programs.

Part 13
Department of Transportation

SECTION 1301 *Résumé of Responsibilities.* The Secretary of Transportation, in carrying out his responsibilities to exercise leadership in transportation matters affecting the national defense and those involving national or regional transportation emergencies, shall prepare emergency plans and develop preparedness programs covering:

(1) Preparation and promulgation of over-all national policies, plans, and procedures related to providing civil transportation of all forms — air, ground, water, and pipelines, including public storage and warehousing (except storage of petroleum and gas and agricultural food resources including cold storage): *Provided* that plans for the movement of petroleum and natural gas through pipelines shall be the responsibility of the Secretary of the Interior except to the extent that such plans are a part of functions vested in the Secretary of Transportation by law;

(2) Movement of passengers and materials of all types by all forms of civil transportation;

(3) Determination of the proper apportionment and allocation for control of the total civil transportation capacity, or any portion thereof, to meet over-all essential civil and military needs;

(4) Determination and identification of the transportation resources available and required to meet all degrees of national emergencies and regional transportation emergencies;

(5) Assistance to the various States, the local political subdivisions thereof, and non-governmental organizations and systems engaged in transportation activities in the preparation of emergency plans;

(6) Rehabilitation and recovery of the Nation's transportation systems; and

(7) Provisions for port security and safety, for aids to maritime navigation, and for search and rescue and law enforcement over, upon, and under the navigable waters of the United States and the high seas.

SEC. 1302 *Transportation Planning and Coordination Functions.* In carrying out the provisions of Section 1301, the Secretary of Transportation, with assistance and support of other Federal, State and local governmental agencies, and the transport industries, as appropriate, shall:

(1) Obtain, assemble, analyze, and evaluate data on current and projected emergency requirements of all claimants for all forms of civil transportation to meet the needs of the military and of the civil economy, and on current and projected civil transportation resources — of all forms — available to the United States to move passengers or materials in an emergency.

(2) Develop plans and procedures to provide — under emergency conditions — for the collection and analysis of passenger and cargo movement demands as they relate to the capabilities of the various forms of transport, including the periodic assessment of over-all transport resources available to meet emergency requirements.

(3) Conduct a continuing analysis of transportation requirements and capabilities in relation to economic projections for the purpose of initiating actions and/or recommending incentive and/or regulatory programs designed to stimulate government and industry improvement of the structure of the transportation system for use in an emergency.

(4) Develop systems for the control of the movement of passengers and cargo by all forms of transportation, except for those resources owned by, controlled by, or under the jurisdiction of the Department of Defense, including allocation of resources and assignment of priorities, and develop policies, standards, and procedures for emergency enforcement of these controls.

SEC. 1303 *Departmental Emergency Transportation Preparedness.* Except for those resources owned by, controlled by, or under the jurisdiction of the Department of Defense, the Secretary of Transportation shall prepare emergency operational plans and programs for, and develop a capability to carry out, the transportation operating responsibilities assigned to the Department, including but not limited to:

(1) Allocating air carrier civil air transportation capacity and equipment to meet civil and military requirements.

(2) Emergency management, including construction, reconstruction, and maintenance of the Nation's civil airports, civil aviation operating facilities, civil aviation services, and civil aircraft (other than air carrier aircraft), except manufacturing facilities.

(3) Emergency management of all Federal, State, city, local, and other highways, roads, streets, bridges, tunnels, and appurtenant structures, including:

(a) The adaptation, development, construction, reconstruction, and maintenance of the Nation's highway and street systems to meet emergency requirements;

(b) The protection of the traveling public by assisting State and local authorities in informing them of the dangers of travel through hazardous areas; and

(c) The regulation of highway traffic in an emergency through a national program in cooperation with all Federal, State, and local governmental units or other agencies concerned.

(4) Emergency plans for urban mass transportation, including:

(a) Providing guidance to urban communities in their emergency mass transportation planning efforts, either directly or through State, regional, or metropolitan agencies;

(b) Coordinating all such emergency planning with the Department of Housing and Urban Development to assure compatibility with emergency plans for all other aspects of urban development;

(c) Maintaining an inventory of urban mass transportation systems.

(5) Maritime safety and law enforcement over, upon, and under the high seas and waters, subject to the jurisdiction of the United States, in the following specific programs:

(a) Safeguarding vessels, harbors, ports, and waterfront facilities from destruction, loss or injury, accidents, or other causes of a similar nature.

(b) Safe passage over, upon, and under the high seas and United States waters through effective and reliable systems of aids to navigation and ocean stations.

(c) Waterborne access to ice-bound locations in furtherance of national economic, scientific, defense, and consumer needs.

(d) Protection of lives, property, natural resources, and national interests through enforcement of Federal law and timely assistance.

(e) Safety of life and property through regulation of commercial vessels, their officers and crew, and administration of maritime safety law.

(f) Knowledge of the sea, its boundaries, and its resources through collection and analysis of data in support of the national interest.

(g) Operational readiness for essential wartime functions.

(6) Planning for the emergency management and opera-

tion of the Alaska Railroad, and for the continuity of railroad and petroleum pipeline safety programs.

(7) Planning for the emergency operation and maintenance of the United States-controlled sections of the Saint Lawrence Seaway.

Part 14
Atomic Energy Commission

SECTION 1401 *Functions.* The Atomic Energy Commission shall prepare national emergency plans and develop preparedness programs for the continuing conduct of atomic energy activities of the Federal Government. These plans and programs shall be designed to develop a state of readiness in these areas with respect to all conditions of national emergency, including attack upon the United States and, consistent with applicable provisions of the Atomic Energy Act of 1954, as amended, shall be closely coordinated with the Department of Defense and the Office of Emergency Preparedness. The Atomic Energy Commission shall:

(1) *Production.* Continue or resume in an emergency, essential (a) manufacture, development, and control of nuclear weapons and equipment, except to the extent that the control over such weapons and equipment shall have been transferred to the Department of Defense; (b) development and technology related to reactors; (c) process development and production of feed material, special nuclear materials, and other special products; (d) related raw materials procurement, processing, and development; and (e) repair, maintenance, and construction related to the above.

(2) *Regulation.* Continue or resume in an emergency (a) controlling the possession, use, transfer, import, and export of atomic materials and facilities; and (b) ordering the operation or suspension of licensed facilities, and recapturing from licensees, where necessary, special nuclear materials whether related to military support or civilian activities.

(3) *Public health and safety.* Shut down, where required, in anticipation of an imminent enemy attack on the United States, and maintain under surveillance, all Commission-owned facilities which could otherwise constitute a significant hazard to public health and safety, and insure the development of appropriate emergency plans for nuclear reactors and other nuclear activities licensed by the Commission whether privately-owned or Government-owned.

(4) *Scentific, technical, and public atomic energy information.* Organize, reproduce, and disseminate appropriate public atomic energy information and scientific and technical reports and data relating to nuclear science research, development, engineering, applications, and effects to interested Government agencies, the scientific and technical communities, and approved, friendly, and cooperating foreign nations.

(5) *International atomic energy affairs.* Maintain, in consultation with the Department of State, essential liaison with foreign nations with respect to activities of mutual interest involving atomic energy.

(6) *Health services.* Assist the Department of Health, Education, and Welfare, consistent with the above requirements, in integrating into civilian health programs in an emergency the Commission's remaining health manpower and facilities not required for the performance of the Commission's essential emergency functions.

(7) *Priorities and allocations.* Plan for the administration of any priorities and allocations authority delegated to the Atomic Energy Commission. Authorize procurement and production schedules and make allotments of controlled materials pursuant to program determinations of the Office of Emergency Preparedness.

Part 15
Civil Aeronautics Board
SECTION 1501 *Definitions.* As used in this part:

(1) "War Air Service Program" (hereinafter referred to as WASP) means the program designed to provide for the maintenance of essential civil air routes and services, and to provide for the distribution and redistribution of air carrier aircraft among civil air transport carriers after withdrawal of aircraft allocated to the Civil Reserve Air Fleet.

(2) "Civil Reserve Air Fleet" (hereinafter referred to as CRAF) means those air carrier aircraft allocated by the Secretary of Transportation to the Department of Defense to meet essential military needs in the event of an emergency.

SEC. 1502 *Functions.* The Civil Aeronautics Board, under the coordinating authority of the Secretary of Transportation, shall:

(1) *Distribution of aircraft.* Develop plans and be prepared to carry out such distribution and redistribution of all air carrier civil aircraft allocated by the Secretary of Transportation among the civil air transport carriers as may be necessary to assure the maintenance of essential civil routes and services under WASP operations after the CRAF requirements have been met.

(2) *Economic regulations.* Develop plans covering route authorizations and operations, tariffs, rates, and fares charged the public, mail rates, government compensation and subsidy, and accounting and contracting procedures essential to WASP operations.

(3) *Operational controls and priorities.* Develop plans and procedures for the administration of operational controls and priorities of passenger and cargo movements in connection with the utilization of air carrier aircraft for WASP purposes in an emergency.

(4) *Investigation.* Maintain the capability to investigate violations of emergency economic regulations affecting air carrier operations.

(5) *Contracting.* Prepare to perform as a contracting

agency, if such an agency is necessary, in connection with distribution and redistribution of aircraft for WASP.

Part 16
Export-Import Bank of the United States

SECTION 1601 *Functions.* (a) Under guidance of the Secretary of the Treasury, the Export-Import Bank shall develop plans for the utilization of the resources of the Bank, or other resources made available to the Bank, in expansion of productive capacity abroad for essential materials, foreign barter arrangements, acquisition of emergency imports, and in support of the domestic economy, or any other plans designed to strengthen the relative position of the Nation and its allies.

(b) In carrying out the guidance functions described above, the Secretary of the Treasury shall consult with the Secretary of State and the Secretary of Commerce as appropriate.

Part 17
Federal Bank Supervisory Agencies

SECTION 1701 *Financial Plans and Programs.* The Board of Governors of the Federal Reserve System, the Comptroller of the Currency, the Federal Home Loan Bank Board, the Farm Credit Administration, and the Federal Deposit Insurance Coorporation shall participate with the Office of Emergency Preparedness, the Department of the Treasury, and other agencies in the formulation of emergency financial and stabilization policies. The heads of such agencies shall, as appropriate, develop emergency plans, programs, and regulations, in consonance with national emergency financial and stabilization plans and policies, to cope with potential economic effects of mobilization or an attack, including, but not limited to, the following:

(1) *Money and credit.* Provision and regulation of money

and credit in accordance with the needs of the economy, including the acquisition, decentralization, and distribution of emergency supplies of currency; the collection of cash items and non-cash items; and the conduct of fiscal agency and foreign operations.

(2) *Financial institutions.* Provision for the continued or resumed operation of banking, savings and loan, and farm credit institutions, including measures for the re-creation of evidence of assets or liabilities destroyed or inaccessible.

(3) *Liquidity.* Provision of liquidity necessary to the continued or resumed operation of banking, savings and loan, credit unions, and farm credit institutions, including those damaged or destroyed by enemy action.

(4) *Cash withdrawals and credit transfers.* Regulation of the withdrawal of currency and the transfer of credits including deposit and share account balances.

(5) *Insurance.* Provision for the assumption and discharge of liability pertaining to insured deposits and insured savings accounts or withdrawable shares in banking and savings and loan institutions destroyed or made insolvent.

SEC. 1702 *Sharing of war losses.* Heads of agencies shall, as appropriate, participate with the Office of Emergency Preparedness and the Department of the Treasury in the development of policies, plans, and procedures for implementation of national policy on sharing war losses.

Part 18

Federal Communications Commission

SECTION 1801 *Definitions.* As used in this part:

(1) "Common carrier" means any person subject to Commission regulation engaged in providing for use by the public, for hire, interstate or foreign communications facilities or services by wire or radio; but a person engaged in radio broadcasting shall not, insofar as such person is so engaged, be deemed a common carrier.

(2) "Broadcast facilities" means those stations licensed by the Commission for the dissemination of radio communications intended to be received by the public directly or by the intermediary of relay stations.

(3) "Safety and special radio services" includes those non-broadcast and non-common carrier services which are licensed by the Commission under the generic designation "safety and special radio services" pursuant to the Commission's Rules and Regulations.

SEC. 1802 *Functions.* The Federal Communications Commission shall develop policies, plans, and procedures, in consonance with national telecommunications plans and policies developed pursuant to Executive Order No. 10705, Executive Order No. 10995, Executive Order No. 11051, the Presidential Memorandum of August 21, 1963, "Establishment of the National Communications System", and other appropriate authority, covering:

(1) *Common carrier service.* (a) Extension, discontinuance, or reduction of common carrier facilities or services, and issuance of appropriate authorizations for such facilities, services, and personnel in an emergency; and control of all rates, charges, practices, classifications, and regulations for service to Government and non-Government users during an emergency, in consonance with overall national economic stabilization policies.

(b) Development and administration of priority systems for public correspondence and for the use and resumption of leased inter-city private line service in an emergency.

(c) Use of common carrier facilities and services to overseas points to meet vital needs in an emergency.

(2) *Broadcasting service.* Construction, activation, or deactivation of broadcasting facilities and services, the continuation or suspension of broadcasting services and facilities, and issuance of appropriate authorizations for such facilities, services, and personnel in an emergency.

44

(3) *Safety and special radio services.* Authorization, operation, and use of safety and special radio services, facilities, and personnel in the national interest in an emergency.

(4) *Radio frequency assignment.* Assignment of radio frequencies to, and their use by, Commission licensees in an emergency.

(5) *Electromagnetic radiation.* Closing of any radio station or any device capable of emitting electro-magnetic radiation or suspension or amending any rules or regulations applicable thereto, in any emergency, except for those belonging to, or operated by, any department or agency of the United States Government.

(6) *Investigation and enforcement.* Investigation of violations of pertinent law and regulations in an emergency, and development of procedures designated to initiate, recommend, or otherwise bring about appropriate enforcement actions required in the interest of national security.

Part 19
Federal Power Commission

SECTION 1901 *Functions.* The Federal Power Commission shall assist the Department of the Interior, in conformity with Part 7, in the preparation of national emergency plans and the development of preparedness programs for electric power and natural gas in the areas as set forth in the Memorandum of Agreement dated August 9, 1962, between the Secretary of the Interior and the Chairman of the Federal Power Commission.

Part 20
General Services Administration

SECTION 2001 *Résumé of Responsibilities.* The Administrator of General Services shall prepare national emergency plans and develop preparedness programs designed to permit modification or expansion of the activities of the General

Services Administration under the Federal Property and Administrative Services Act of 1949, as amended and other statutes prescribing the duties and responsibilities of the Administrator. These plans and programs shall include, but not be limited to: (1) operation, maintenance, and protection of Federal buildings and their sites; construction, alteration, and repair of public buildings; and acquisition, utilization, and disposal of real and personal properties; (2) public utilities service management for Federal agencies; (3) telecommunications to meet the essential requirements of civilian activities of executive departments and agencies; (4) transportation management to meet the traffic service requirements of civilian activities of Federal agencies; (5) records management; (6) Emergency Federal Register; (7) Government-wide supply support; (8) service to survival items stockpiles; (9) national industrial reserve; (10) guidance and consultation to Government agencies regarding facilities protection measures; (11) administration of assigned functions under the Defense Production Act; and (12) administration and operation of the stockpile of strategic and critical materials in accordance with policies and guidance furnished by the Office of Emergency Preparedness.

SEC. 2002 *Functions.* The Administrator of General Services shall:

(1) *Public buildings.* Develop emergency plans and procedures for the operation, maintenance, and protection of both existing and new Federally-owned and Federally-occupied buildings, and construction, alteration, and repair of public buildings. Develop emergency operating procedures for the control, acquisition, assignment, and priority of occupancy of real property by the Federal Government and by State and local governments to the extent they may be performing functions as agents of the Federal Government.

(2) *Public utility service management.* Develop emergency operational plans and procedures for the claimancy, procure-

ment, and use of public utility services for emergency activities of executive agencies of the Government.

(3) *Communications.* Plan for and provide, operate, and maintain appropriate telecommunications facilities designed to meet the essential requirements of Federal civilian departments and agencies during an emergency within the framework of the National Communications System. Plans and programs of the Administrator shall be in consonance with national telecommunications policies, plans, and programs developed pursuant to Executive Order No. 10705, Executive Order No. 10995, Executive Order No. 11051, and the Presidential Memorandum of August 21, 1963, "Establishment of the National Communications System," or other appropriate authority.

(4) *Transportation.* Develop plans and procedures for providing: (a) general transportation and traffic management services to civilian activities of Federal agencies in connection with movement of property and supplies, including the claimancy, contracting, routing, and accounting of Government shipments by commercial transportation in time of emergency; and (b) motor vehicle service to meet the administrative needs of Federal agencies, including dispatch and scheduled Government motor service at and between headquarters, field offices, relocation sites, and other installations of the Federal and State governments.

(5) *Records.* Provide instructions and advice on appraisal, selection, preservation, arrangement, reference, reproduction, storage, and salvage of essential records needed for the operation of the Federal Government after attack, on an emergency basis, including a decentralized system.

(6) *Federal Register.* Develop emergency procedures for providing and making available, on a decentralized basis, a Federal Register of Presidential Proclamations and Executive Orders, Federal administrative regulations, Federal emergency notices and actions, and Acts of Congress during a national emergency.

(7) *Government-wide procurement and supply.* Prepare plans and procedures for the coordination and/or operation of Government-wide supply programs to meet the requirements of Federal agencies under emergency conditions, including the development of policies, methods, and procedures for emergency procurement and for emergency requisitioning of private property when authorized by law and competent authority; identification of essential civil agency supply items under the Federal catalog system; development of emergency Federal specifications and standards; determination of sources of supply; procurement of personal property and non-personal services; furnishing appropriate inspection and contract administration services; and establishment, coordination, and/or operation of emergency storage and distribution facilities.

(8) *Survival item stockpiles.* Assist the Department of Health, Education, and Welfare, insofar as civil defense medical stockpile items under its jurisdiction are concerned, and the Department of Defense, insofar as survival items under its jurisdiction are concerned, in formulating plans and programs for service activity support relating to stockpiling of such supplies and equipment. The Administrator shall arrange for the procurement, storage, maintenance, inspection, survey, withdrawal, and disposal of supplies and equipment in accordance with the provisions of interagency agreements with the departments concerned.

(9) *National industrial reserve and machine tool program.* Develop plans for the custody of the industrial plants and production equipment in the national industrial reserve and assist the Department of Defense, in collaboration with the Department of Commerce, in the development of plans and procedures for the disposition, emergency reactivation, and utilization of the plants and equipment of this reserve in the custody of the Administrator.

(10) *Excess and surplus real and personal property.* Devel-

op plans and emergency operating procedures for the utilization of excess and surplus real and personal property by Federal Government agencies with emergency assignments or by State and local governmental units as directed, including review of the property holdings of Federal agencies which do not possess emergency functions to determine the availability of property for emergency use, and including the disposal of real and personal property and the rehabilitation of personal property.

(11) *Facilities protection and building and shelter manager service.* In accordance with the guidance from the Department of Defense, promote, with respect to Federal buildings and installations, a Government-wide program (a) to stimulate protection, preparedness, and control in emergencies in order to minimize the effects of overt or covert attack, including dispersal of facilities; and (b) to establish shelter manager organizations, including safety and service personnel, shelter manager service, first aid, police, and evacuation service.

SEC. 2003 *Defense Production.* The Administrator of General Services shall assist the Office of Emergency Preparedness in the formulation of plans and programs relating to the certification of procurement programs, subsidy payments, and plant improvement programs provided for by the Defense Production Act of 1950, as amended.

SEC. 2004 *Strategic and Critical Materials Stockpiles.* The Administrator of General Services shall assist the Office of Emergency Preparedness in formulating plans, programs, and reports relating to the stockpiling of strategic and critical materials. Within these plans and programs, the Administrator shall provide for the procurement (for this purpose, procurement includes upgrading, rotation, and beneficiation), storage, security, maintenance, inspection, withdrawal, and disposal of materials, supplies, and equipment.

Part 21
Interstate Commerce Commission

SECTION 2101 *Résumé of Responsibilities.* The Chairman of the Interstate Commerce Commission, under the coordinating authority of the Secretary of Transportation, shall prepare national emergency plans and develop preparedness programs covering railroad utilization, reduction of vulnerability, maintenance, restoration, and operation in an emergency (other than for the Alaska Railroad — see Section 1303(6)); motor carrier utilization, reduction of vulnerability, and operation in an emergency; inland waterway utilization of equipment and shipping, reduction of vulnerability, and operation in an emergency; and also provide guidance and consultation to domestic surface transportation and storage industries, as defined below, regarding emergency preparedness measures, and to States regarding development of their transportation plans in assigned areas.

SEC. 2102 *Definitions.* As used in this part:

(1) "Domestic surface transportation and storage" means rail, motor, and inland water transportation facilities and services and public storage;

(2) "Public storage" includes warehouses and other places which are used for the storage of property belonging to persons other than the persons having the ownership or control of such premises;

(3) "Inland water transportation" includes shipping on all inland waterways and Great Lakes shipping engaged solely in the transportation of passengers or cargo between United States ports on the Great Lakes;

(4) Specifically excluded, for the purposes of this part, are pipelines, petroleum and gas storage, agricultural food resources storage, including the cold storage of food resources, the St. Lawrence Seaway, ocean ports and Great Lakes ports and port facilities, highways, streets, roads, bridges, and related appurtenances, maintenance of inland waterways, and

50

any transportation owned by or pre-allocated to the military.

SEC. 2103 *Transportation Functions.* The Interstate Commerce Commission shall:

(1) *Operational control.* Develop plans with appropriate private transportation and storage organizations and associations for the coordination and direction of the use of domestic surface transportation and storage facilities for movement of passenger and freight traffic.

(2) *Emergency operations.* Develop and maintain necessary orders and regulations for the operation of domestic surface transport and storage industries in an emergency.

Part 22
National Aeronautics and Space Administration

SECTION 2201 *Functions.* The Administrator of the National Aeronautics and Space Administration shall:

(1) *Research and development.* Adapt and utilize the scientific and technological capability of the National Aeronautics and Space Administration, consistent with over-all requirements to meet priority needs of the programs of the Federal Government in an emergency. This will include the direction and conduct of essential research and development activities relating to (a) aircraft, spacecraft, and launch vehicles, (b) associated instrumentation, guidance, control and payload, propulsion, and communications systems, (c) scientific phenomena affecting both manned and unmanned space flights, (d) the life sciences (biology, medicine, and psychology) as they apply to aeronautics and space, and (e) atmospheric and geophysical sciences.

(2) *Military support.* Provide direct assistance as requested by the Department of Defense and other agencies in support of the military effort. This may include (a) undertaking urgent projects to develop superior aircraft, spacecraft, launch vehicles, and weapons systems, (b) developing

methods to counter novel or revolutionary enemy weapons systems. (c) providing technical advice and assistance on matters involving air and space activities, and (d) furnishing personnel and facilities to assist in emergency repairs of equipment deficiencies and for other essential purposes.

Part 23
National Science Foundation

SECTION 2301 *Functions.* The Director of the National Science Foundation shall:

(1) *Manpower functions.* Assist the Department of Labor in sustaining readiness for the mobilization of civilian manpower by: (a) maintaining the Foundation's register of scientific and technical personnel in such form and at such locations as will assure maximum usefulness in an emergency; (b) being prepared for rapid expansion of the Foundation's current operation as a central clearing house for information covering all scientific and technical personnel in the United States and its possessions; and (c) developing, in consultation with the Department of Labor, the Selective Service System, the Department of Defense, and the Office of Science and Technology, plans and procedures to assure the most effective distribution and utilization of the Nation's scientific and engineering manpower in an emergency.

(2) *Special functions.* (a) Provide leadership in developing, with the assistance of Federal and State agencies and appropriate non-governmental organizations, the ability to mobilize scientists, in consonance with over-all civilian manpower mobilization programs, to perform or assist in performance of special tasks, including the identification of and defense against unconventional warfare; (b) advance the national radiological defense capability by including, in consultation with appropriate agencies, pertinent scientific information and radiological defense techniques in the Foundation's scientific institute program for science, mathe-

matics, and engineering teachers; (c) assemble data on the location and character of major scientific research facilities, including non-governmental as well as government facilities, and their normal inventories of types of equipment and instruments which would be useful in identification and analysis of hazards to human life in the aftermath of enemy attack; and (d) prepare to carry on necessary programs for basic research and for training of scientific manpower.

Part 24
Railroad Retirement Board

SECTION 2401 *Functions.* The Railroad Retirement Board shall:

(1) *Manpower functions.* Within the framework of the over-all manpower plans and programs of the Department of Labor, assist in the mobilization of civilian manpower in an emergency by developing plans for the recruitment and referral of that segment of the Nation's manpower recources subject to the Railroad Retirement and Railroad Unemployment Insurance Acts.

(2) *Benefit payments.* Develop plans for administering, under emergency conditions, the essential aspects of the Railroad Retirement Act and Railroad Unemployment Insurance Act consistent with overall Federal plans for the continuation of benefit payments after an enemy attack.

Part 25
Securities and Exchange Commission

SECTION 2501 *Functions.* The Securities and Exchange Commission shall collaborate with the Secretary of the Treasury in the development of emergency financial control plans, programs, procedures, and regulations for:

(1) *Stock trading.* Temporary closure of security exchanges, suspension of redemption rights, and freezing of

stock and bond prices, if required in the interest of maintaining economic controls.

(2) *Modified trading.* Development of plans designed to reestablish and maintain a stable and orderly market for securities when the situation permits under emergency conditions.

(3) *Protection of securities.* Provision of a national records system which will make it possible to establish current ownership of securities in the event major trading centers and depositories are destroyed.

(4) *Flow of capital.* The control of the formation and flow of private capital as it relates to new securities offerings or expansion of prior offerings for the purpose of establishing or reestablishing industries in relation to the Nation's needs in or following a national emergency.

(5) *Flight of capital.* The prevention of the flight of capital outside this country, in coordination with the Secretary of Commerce, and the impounding of securities in the hands of enemy aliens.

Part 26
Small Business Administration

SECTION 2601 *Functions.* The Administrator of the Small Business Administration shall:

(1) *Prime contract authority.* Develop plans to administer a program for the acquisition of prime contracts by the Administration and, in turn, for negotiating or otherwise letting of subcontracts to capable small business concerns in an emergency.

(2) *Resource information.* Provide data on facilities, inventories, and potential production capacity of small business concerns to all interested agencies.

(3) *Procurement.* Develop plans to determine jointly with Federal procurement agencies, as appropriate, which defense contracts are to go to small business concerns and to

certify to the productive and financial ability of small concerns to perform specific contracts, as required.

(4) *Loans for plant modernization.* Develop plans for providing emergency assistance to essential individual industrial establishments through direct loans or participation loans for the financing of production facilities and equipment.

(5) *Resource pools.* Develop plans for encouraging and approving small business defense production and research and development pools.

(6) *Financial assistance.* Develop plans to make loans, directly or in participation with private lending institutions, to small business concerns and to groups or pools of such concerns, to small business investment companies, and to State and local development companies to provide them with funds for lending to small business concerns, for defense and essential civilian purposes.

Part 27
Tennessee Valley Authority

SECTION 2701 *Functions.* The Board of Directors of the Tennessee Valley Authority shall:

(1) *Electric power.* Assist the Department of the Interior in the development of plans for the integration of the Tennessee Valley Authority power system into national emergency programs and prepare plans for the emergency management, operation, and maintenance of the system and for its essential expansion.

(2) *Waterways.* Assist the Interstate Commerce Commission, under the coordinating authority of the Secretary of Transportation, in the development of plans for integration and control of inland waterway transportation systems and, in cooperation with the Department of Defense and the Department of the Interior, prepare plans for the management, operation, and maintenance of the river control system

in the Tennessee River and certain of its tributaries for navigation during an emergency.

(3) *Flood control.* Develop plans and maintain its river control operations for the prevention or control of floods caused by natural phenomena or overt and covert attack affecting the Tennessee River System and, in so doing, collaborate with the Department of Defense with respect to the control of water in the lower Ohio and Mississippi Rivers.

(4) *Emergency health services and sanitary water supplies.* Assist the Department of Health, Education, and Welfare in the development of plans and programs covering emergency health services, civilian health manpower, and health resources in the Tennessee Valley Authority area and, in collaboration with the Department of the Interior and the Department of Health, Education, and Welfare, prepare plans for the management, operation, and maintenance of the Tennessee River System consistent with the needs for sanitary public water supplies, waste disposal, and vector control.

(5) *Coordination of water use.* Develop plans for determining or proposing priorities for the use of water by the Tennessee Valley Authority in the event of conflicting claims arising from the functions listed above.

(6) *Fertilizer.* Assist the Department of Agriculture in the development of plans for the distribution and claimancy of fertilizer; assist the Department of Commerce and the Department of Defense in the development of Tennessee Valley Authority production quotas and any essential expansion of production facilities, and prepare plans for the management, operation, and maintenance of its facilities for the manufacture of nitrogen and phosphorous fertilizers.

(7) *Munitions production.* Perform chemical research in munitions as requested by the Department of Defense, maintain standby munitions production facilities, and develop plans for converting and utilizing fertilizer facilities as

required in support of the Department of Defense's munitions program.

(8) *Land management.* Develop plans for the maintenance, management, and utilization of Tennessee Valley Authority-controlled lands in the interest of an emergency economy.

(9) *Food and forestry.* Assist the Department of Agriculture in the development of plans for the harvesting and processing of fish and game, and the Department of Commerce in the development of plans for the production and processing of forest products.

(10) *Coordination with Valley States.* Prepare plans and agreements with Tennessee Valley States, consistent with Federal programs, for appropriate integration of Tennessee Valley Authority and State plans for the use of available Tennessee Valley Authority resources.

Part 28
United States Civil Service Commission
SECTION 2801 *Functions.* The United States Civil Service Commission shall:

(1) *Personnel system.* Prepare plans for adjusting the Federal civilian personnel system to simplify administration and to meet emergency demands.

(2) *Utilization.* Develop policies and implementing procedures designed to assist Federal agencies in achieving the most effective utilization of the Federal Government's civilian manpower in an emergency.

(3) *Manpower policies.* As the representative of the Federal Government as an employer, participate, as appropriate, in the formulation of national and regional manpower policies as they affect Federal civilian personnel and establish implementing policies as necessary.

(4) *Manpower administration.* Prepare plans, in consonance with national manpower policies and programs, for the

administration of emergency civilian manpower and employment policies within the executive branch of the Government, including the issuance and enforcement of regulations to implement such policies.

(5) *Wage and salary stabilization.* Participate, as appropriate, with the Office of Emergency Preparedness and the Department of Labor in the formulation of national and regional wage and salary stabilization policies as they affect Federal civilian personnel. Within the framework of such policies, prepare plans for the implementation of such policies and controls established for employees within the executive branch of the Government, including the issuance and enforcement of necessary regulations.

(6) *Assistance.* Develop plans for rendering personnel management and staffing assistance to new and expanding Federal agencies.

(7) *Recruiting.* Develop plans for the coordination and control of civilian recruiting policies and practices by all Federal agencies in order to increase the effectiveness of the total recruitment efforts during an emergency and to prevent undesirable recruitment practices.

(8) *Reassignment.* Develop plans to facilitate the reassignment or transfer of Federal civilian employees, including the movement of employees from one agency or location to another agency or location, in order to meet the most urgent needs of the executive branch during an emergency.

(9) *Registration.* Develop plans and procedures for a nationwide system of post-attack registration of Federal employees to provide a means for locating and returning to duty those employees who become physically separated from their agencies after an enemy attack, and to provide for the maximum utilization of the skills of surviving employees.

(10) *Deferment.* Develop plans and procedures for a system to control Government requests for the selective service deferment of employees in the executive branch of

the Federal Government and in the municipal government of the District of Columbia.

(11) *Investigation.* Prepare plans, in coordination with agencies having responsibilities in the personnel security field, for the conduct of national agency checks and inquiries, limited suitability investigations, and full field investigations under emergency conditions.

(12) *Salaries, wages, and benefits.* Develop plans for operating under emergency conditions the essential aspects of salary and wage systems and such benefit systems as the Federal Employees Retirement System, the Federal Employees Group Life Insurance Program, the Federal Employees and Retired Federal Employees Health Benefits Programs, and the Federal Employees Compensation Program.

(13) *Federal manpower mobilization.* Assist Federal agencies in establishing manpower plans to meet their own emergency manpower requirements; identify major or special manpower problems of individual Federal agencies and the Federal Government as a whole in mobilizing a civilian work force to meet essential emergency requirements; identify sources of emergency manpower supply for all agencies where manpower problems are indicated; and develop Government-wide plans for the use of surplus Federal civilian manpower.

(14) *Distribution of manpower.* Participate in the formulation of policies and decisions on the distribution of the nation's civilian manpower resources, obtain appropriate civilian manpower data from Federal agencies, and establish necessary implementing policies and procedures within the Executive Branch.

(15) *Training.* Develop, organize, and conduct, as appropriate, interagency training programs in emergency personnel management for Federal employees.

Part 29
Veterans Administration

SECTION 2901 *Functions.* The Administrator of Veterans Affairs shall develop policies, plans, and procedures for the performance of emergency functions with respect to the continuation or restoration of authorized programs of the Veterans Administration under all conditions of national emergency, including attack upon the United States. These include:

(1) The emergency conduct of inpatient and outpatient care and treatment in Veterans Administration medical facilities and participation with the Departments of Defense and Health, Education, and Welfare as provided for in interagency agreements.

(2) The emergency conduct of compensation, pension, rehabilitation, education, and insurance payments consistent with over-all Federal plans for the continuation of Federal benefit payments.

(3) The emergency performance of insurance and loan guaranty functions in accordance with indirect stabilization policies and controls designed to deal with various emergency conditions.

Part 30
General Provisions

SECTION 3001 *Resource Management.* In consonance with the national preparedness, security, and mobilization readiness plans, programs, and operations of the Office of Emergency Preparedness under Executive Order No. 11051 of September 27, 1962, and subject to the provisions of the preceding parts, the head of each department and agency shall:

(1) *Priorities and allocations.* Develop systems for the emergency application of priorities and allocations to the production, distribution, and use of resources for which he has been assigned responsibility.

(2) *Requirements.* Assemble, develop as appropriate, and evaluate requirements for assigned resources, taking into account estimated needs for military, atomic energy, civilian, and foreign purposes. Such evaluation shall take into consideration geographical distribution of requirements under emergency conditions.

(3) *Evaluation.* Assess assigned resources in order to estimate availability from all sources under an emergency situation, analyze resource availabilities in relation to estimated requirements, and develop appropriate recommendations and programs, including those necessary for the maintenance of an adequate mobilization base. Provide data and assistance before and after attack for national resource analysis purposes of the Office of Emergency Preparedness.

(4) *Claimancy.* Prepare plans to claim from the appropriate agency supporting materials, manpower, equipment, supplies, and services which would be needed to carry out assigned responsibilities and other essential functions of his department or agency, and cooperate with other agencies in developing programs to insure availability of such resources in an emergency.

SEC. 3002 *Facilities protection and warfare effects monitoring and reporting.* In consonance with the national preparedness, security, and mobilization readiness plans, programs, and operations of the Office of Emergency Preparedness under Executive Order No. 11051, and with the national civil defense plans, programs, and operations of the Department of Defense under Executive Order No. 10952, the head of each department and agency shall:

(1) *Facilities protection.* Provide facilities protection guidance material adapted to the needs of the facilities and services concerned and promote a national program to stimulate disaster preparedness and control in order to minimize the effects of overt and covert attack on facilities or other resources for which he has management responsi-

61

bility. Guidance shall include, but not be limited to, organization and training of facility employees, personnel shelter, evacuation plans, records protection, continuity of management, emergency repair, dispersal of facilities, and mutual aid associations for an emergency.

(2) *Warfare effects monitoring and reporting.* Maintain a capability, both at national and field levels, to estimate the effects of attack on assigned resources and to collaborate with and provide data to the Office of Emergency Preparedness, the Department of Defense, and other agencies, as appropriate, in verifying and updating estimates of resource status through exchanges of data and mutual assistance, and provide for the detection, identification, monitoring and reporting of such warfare effects at selected facilities under his operation or control.

(3) *Salvage and rehabilitation.* Develop plans for salvage, decontamination, and rehabilitation of facilities involving resources under his jurisdiction.

(4) *Shelter.* In conformity with national shelter policy, where authorized to engage in building construction, plan, design, and construct such buildings to protect the public to the maximum extent feasible against the hazards that could result from an attack upon the United States with nuclear weapons; and where empowered to extend Federal financial assistance, encourage recipients of such financial assistance to use standards for planning design and construction which will maximize protection for the public.

SEC. 3003 *Critical skills and occupations.* (a) The Secretaries of Defense, Commerce, and Labor shall carry out the mandate of the National Security Council, dated February 15, 1968, to "maintain a continuing surveillance over the Nation's manpower needs and identify any particular occupation or skill that may warrant qualifying for deferment on a uniform national basis." In addition, the Secretaries of Defense, Commerce, Labor, and Health, Education, and

62

Welfare shall carry out the mandate of the National Security Council to "maintain a continuing surveillance over the Nation's manpower and education needs to identify any area of graduate study that may warrant qualifying for deferment in the national interest." In carrying out these functions, the Secretaries concerned shall consult with the National Science Foundation with respect to scientific manpower requirements.

(b) The Secretaries of Commerce and Labor shall maintain and issue, as necessary, lists of all essential activities and critical occupations that may be required for emergency preparedness purposes.

SEC. 3004 *Research.* Within the framework of research policies and objectives established by the Office of Emergency Preparedness, the head of each department and agency shall supervise or conduct research in areas directly concerned with carrying out emergency preparedness responsibilities, designate representatives for necessary ad hoc or task force groups, and provide advice and assistance to other agencies in planning for research in areas involving each agency's interest.

SEC. 3005 *Stockpiles.* The head of each department and agency, with appropriate emergency responsibilities, shall assist the Office of Emergency Preparedness in formulating and carrying out plans for stockpiling of strategic and critical materials, and survival items.

SEC. 3006 *Direct Economic Controls.* The head of each department and agency shall cooperate with the Office of Emergency Preparedness and the Federal financial agencies in the development of emergency preparedness measures involving emergency financial and credit measures, as well as price, rent, wage and salary stabilization, and consumer rationing programs.

SEC. 3007 *Financial Aid.* The head of each department and agency shall develop plans and procedures in cooperation with the Federal financial agencies for financial and credit assistance to those segments of the private sector for which he is responsible in the event such assistance is needed under emergency conditions.

SEC. 3008 *Functional Guidance.* The head of each department and agency in carrying out the functions assigned to him by this order, shall be guided by the following:

(1) *National program guidance.* In consonance with the national preparedness, security, and mobilization readiness plans, programs, and operations of the Office of Emergency Preparedness under Executive Order No. 11051, and with the national civil defense plans, programs, and operations of the Department of Defense, technical guidance shall be provided to State and local governments and instrumentalities thereof, to the end that all planning concerned with functions assigned herein will be effectively coordinated. Relations with the appropriate segment of the private sector shall be maintained to foster mutual understanding of Federal emergency plans.

(2) *Interagency coordination.* Emergency preparedness functions shall be coordinated by the head of the department or agency having primary responsibility with all other departments and agencies having supporting functions related thereto.

(3) *Emergency preparedness.* Emergency plans, programs, and an appropriate state of readiness, including organizational readiness, shall be developed as an integral part of the continuing activities of each department or agency on the basis that that department or agency will have the responsibility for carrying out such plans and programs during an emergency. The head of each department or agency shall be prepared to implement all appropriate plans developed under this order. Modifications and temporary organizational changes, based on emergency conditions, shall be in accordance with policy determinations by the President.

(4) *Professional liaison.* Mutual understanding and support of emergency preparedness activities shall be fostered, and the National Defense Executive Reserve shall be promoted by maintaining relations with the appropriate non-governmental sectors.

SEC. 3009 *Training.* The head of each department and agency shall develop and direct training programs which incorporate emergency preparedness and civil defense training and information programs necessary to insure the optimum operational effectiveness of assigned resources, systems, and facilities.

SEC. 3010 *Emergency Public Information.* In consonance with such emergency public information plans and central program decisions of the Office of Emergency Preparedness, and with plans, programs, and procedures established by the Department of Defense to provide continuity of programming for the Emergency Broadcast System, the head of each department and agency shall:

(1) Obtain and provide information as to the emergency functions or assignments of the individual department or agency for dissemination to the American people during the emergency, in accordance with arrangements made by the Office of Emergency Preparedness.

(2) Determine requirements and arrange for prerecordings to provide continuity of program service over the Emergency Broadcast System so that the American people can receive information, advice, and guidance pertaining to the implementation of the civil defense and emergency preparedness plans or assignments of each individual department or agency.

SEC. 3011 *Emergency Actions.* This order does not confer authority to put into effect any emergency plan, procedure, policy, program, or course of action prepared or developed pursuant to this order. Plans so developed may be effectuated only in the event that authority for such effectuation is provided by a law enacted by the Congress or by an order or directive issued by the President pursuant to statutes or the Constitution of the United States.

SEC. 3012 *Redelegation.* The head of each department and agency is hereby authorized to redelegate the functions assigned to him by this order, and to authorize successive redelegations to agencies or instrumentalities of the United States, and to officers and employees of the United States.

SEC. 3013 *Transfer of Functions.* Any emergency preparedness function under this order, or parts thereof, may be transferred from one department or agency to another with the consent of the heads of the organizations involved and with the concurrence of the Director of the Office of Emergency Preparedness. Any new emergency preparedness function may be assigned to the head of a department or agency by the Director of the Office of Emergency Preparedness by mutual consent.

SEC. 3014 *Retention of Existing Authority.* Except as provided by Section 3015, nothing in this order shall be deemed to derogate from any now existing assignment of functions to any department or agency or officer thereof made by statute, Executive order, or Presidential directives, including Memoranda.

SEC. 3015 *Revoked Orders.* The following are hereby revoked:

(1) Defense Mobilization Order VI-2 of December 11, 1953.

(2) Defense Mobilization Order I-12 of October 5, 1954.

(3) Executive Order No. 10312 of December 10, 1951.

(4) Executive Order No. 10346 of April 17, 1952.

(5) Executive Order No. 10997 of February 16, 1962.

(6) Executive Order No. 10998 of February 16, 1962.

(7) Executive Order No. 10999 of February 16, 1962.

(8) Executive Order No. 11000 of February 16, 1962.

(9) Executive Order No. 11001 of February 16, 1962.

(10) Executive Order No. 11002 of February 16, 1962.
(11) Executive Order No. 11003 of February 16, 1962.
(12) Executive Order No. 11004 of February 16, 1962.
(13) Executive Order No. 11005 of February 16, 1962.
(14) Executive Order No. 11087 of February 26, 1963.
(15) Executive Order No. 11088 of February 26, 1963.
(16) Executive Order No. 11089 of February 26, 1963.
(17) Executive Order No. 11090 of February 26, 1963.
(18) Executive Order No. 11091 of February 26, 1963.
(19) Executive Order No. 11092 of February 26, 1963.
(20) Executive Order No. 11093 of February 26, 1963.
(21) Executive Order No. 11094 of February 26, 1963.
(22) Executive Order No. 11095 of February 26, 1963.
(23) Executive Order No. 11310 of October 11, 1966.

THE WHITE HOUSE,
October 28, 1969.

(signed) Richard Nixon

[F.R. Doc. 68-13005; Filed, Oct. 28, 1969; 2:19 p.m.]

Also Available From Western Islands

Richard Nixon: The Man Behind The Mask
   by Gary Allen, $8.00 hardbound, $2.00 paperbound. .

Nixon's Palace Guard
   by Gary Allen, $2.00 paperbound.

Teddy Bare: The Last Of The Kennedy Clan
   by Zad Rust, $7.00 hardbound, $2.00 paperbound.

Fabian Freeway: High Road To Socialism In The U.S.A.
   by Rose Martin, $4.95 hardbound.

The Fearful Master: A Second Look At The United Nations
   by G. Edward Griffin, $5.00 hardbound, $2.00 paperbound,
   $1.00 pocketsize.

It's Very Simple: The True Story Of Civil Rights
   by Alan Stang, $5.00 hardbound, $.75 paperbound.